REREADING LITERATURE
Alfred Tennyson

REREADING LITERATURE
General Editor: Terry Eagleton

Alexander Pope
Laura Brown

Charles Dickens
Steven Connor

Emily Brontë
James H. Kavanagh

W. H. Auden
Stan Smith

William Blake
Edward Larrissy

Alfred Tennyson
Alan Sinfield

William Shakespeare
Terry Eagleton

Geoffrey Chaucer
Stephen Knight

Alfred Tennyson

Alan Sinfield

Basil Blackwell

First published 1986

Basil Blackwell Ltd
108 Cowley Road, Oxford OX4 1JF, UK

Basil Blackwell Inc.
432 Park Avenue South, Suite 1505,
New York, NY 10016, USA

British Library Cataloguing in Publication Data

Sinfield, Alan
   Alfred Tennyson – (Rereading literature)
   1. Tennyson, Alfred Tennyson, *Baron* – Criticism
   and interpretation.
   I. Title   II. Series
   821′.8   PR5588

ISBN 0–631–13582–0
ISBN 0–631–13583–9 Pbk

Library of Congress Cataloging in Publication Data

Sinfield, Alan
   Alfred Tennyson.
   (Rereading literature)
   Bibliography: p.
   Includes index.
   1. Tennyson, Alfred Tennyson, Baron, 1809–1892–
Criticism and interpretation. I. Title. II. Series:
Re-reading literature.
PR5588.S53   1986   821′.8   85–18693
ISBN 0–631–13582–0
ISBN 0–631–13583–9 (pbk.)

C.2

59,270

Typeset by Oxford Publishing Services
Printed and Bound in Great Britain by
T.J. Press (Padstow) Ltd, Padstow, Cornwall

In memory of Lucy Sinfield
1912–1985

Mr Tennyson, reading 'In Memoriam' to his Sovereign
(from *The Poets' Corner*, 1904, by Max Beerbohm, reproduced by kind permission of
the British Library)

Contents

Editor's Preface

Tennyson was the last major 'public' poet in England, with a popularity for which the contemporary parallel would be less a poet than a pop star. But he also wrote at a time when, as Alan Sinfield points out in this study, poetry itself was becoming rapidly 'marginalized', banished to the periphery of a crassly utilitarian society. Tennyson is thus at once a poet of the 'centre' and the 'margins': on the one hand poet laureate, spokesman for conservative values and Victorian patriarch; on the other hand a radically alienated, deeply subjective refugee from the march of bourgeois progress, whose 'feminine' sensuousness finds its nourishment in the privatized and exotic. The visionary, prophetic, representative role of the early Romantic poet continues to haunt his work, but now increasingly emptied of its political content. By the time of Tennyson, the imagination has ceased to be, as it was for the early Romantics, a radical political force; hence the painful paradoxes of a poetry which hymns 'freedom' in rhapsodic style but remains firmly wedded to the central values of an exploitative social order. That social order, and the marginal, subjective poetry which embroiders it, are finally sides of the same coin.

As Sinfield shows, the anxieties of a rapidly secularizing, industrializing society whose culture lies under the threat of anarchy trace themselves through Tennyson's work in the form of a crisis of language. It is a notable contradiction of industrial capitalist society that it needs to call for its ideological stability on the very absolute spiritual values which materialism and secularization themselves put into question. Tennyson's language thus opens up a troubling gap between itself and some ultimate reality it can never quite encompass, doubling back upon itself in the process to become itself a kind of material, densely textured 'thing'. As the poet strives to 'fill' the sign with its object, render the material world in all its sensuous presence, what he gives us, paradoxically, is not the world itself so much as language, which now comes to stand in, fetish-like, for the reality which ceaselessly eludes it. Perhaps the most scandalous recognition for a society which invests so deeply in the individual self is that this, too, can be viewed as a complex effect of language; and Sinfield demonstrates how Tennyson is at once gloomily alert to this possibility and yet still resolute in his striving for a Truth which would transcend all discourse.

If the individual self is one term of the Tennysonian equation, the other is the 'universal'. Between them, as this study shows, they manage to elide the political and historical dimension which is where Tennyson's problems have their real home. Few readers or critics are now likely to credit the ludicrous claim that a particular Victorian middle-class conservative was speaking in *In Memoriam* in the language of the human race itself; but this abstract coupling of the 'individual' and 'universal', fiercely hostile to the social roots of identity, continues to exert its implacable influence over contemporary literary criticism. One major element of the social roots of identity is, of course, sexuality; and this study is more searching and detailed than most in its examination of the sliding and troubling of gender roles in such major Tennyson poems as *The Princess* and *In Memoriam*. In doing so, it elicits a fascinating 'sub-text' beneath Tennyson's work, which is one reason why his poetry can still speak significantly to us today.

Terry Eagleton

1 The Relevance of Tennyson

Tennyson's poetry found a direct response with very many of his contemporaries. Samuel Bamford, self-educated Lancashire handloom weaver, author of *The Life of a Radical*, wrote to Tennyson in 1849: 'Your poems, I cannot forget them. I cannot put them away from my thoughts; the persons and scenes they represent haunt me.' Queen Victoria told Tennyson: 'Next to the Bible *In Memoriam* is my comfort.' When he published *Maud* a reader wrote anonymously: 'Sir, – I used to worship you, but now I hate you. I loathe and detest you. You beast! So you've taken to imitating Longfellow. Yours in aversion . . . '.[1] For and against, readers found Tennyson moving, controversial, culturally central.

Subsequent readers have constructed their own relationships with Tennyson's poetry. In this chapter I will discuss three ways of attempting this. One is established in literary criticism, a second is often proposed by student readers, the third is the mode of this book.

Established literary criticism has generally assumed that great Literature (by definition) transcends the conditions of its origin and embodies universal and eternal truths about humankind. Victorian literary critics also suggested this. Tennyson's friend, James Spedding, reviewing *Poems* (1842), declared: 'All that is of true and lasting worth in poetry, must have its root in a sound view of human life and the condition of man in the world.'[2] If this thought is well founded, then Tennyson will be important to readers today because of the enduring profundity of his writing; criticism works to secure this end. However, such claims to essential and absolute truth are, in effect if not in intention, strategies tending to assert one world view over others. The way this can work may be readily observed in a rather clumsy instance. F. J. Rowe and W. T. Webb introduced a selection of Tennyson's poems for schools in 1938 in these terms: 'The emotions that he appeals to are generally easy to understand and common to all ... The moral laws which he so strongly upholds are those primary sanctions upon which average English society is founded.'[3] The slide here from 'common to all' to 'average English society' now seems blatant. Universal truth is identified with the wisdom of particular social arrangements. In fact, these editors were professors of English Literature at Presidency College, Calcutta, one of the breeding grounds of radical Indian nationalism, so their assertion that Tennyson exercises a 'powerful charm ... over the hearts and minds of all English speaking peoples' (p. x) – all? – can be seen both as a justification of cultural imperialism and as wishful thinking.

Latterly things have been managed more subtly, as in this instance by Clyde de L. Ryals:

> In the *Idylls* Tennyson takes into account all the contradictions of existence. For the poem represents existence as blossoming in eternity but accomplished in the instant; it portrays that existence as choice and expectation, risk and gain, life and death, the past declaring itself in the present; and finally it shows life as a permanent tension between the finite and the infinite.[4]

Two things are happening here. First, the distinctive Victorian character of *Idylls of the King*, which no doubt interferes with their significance for modern readers, is effaced. For Victorians, the importance of these poems derived from their apparent concern with Christian sexual morality. Dean Alford, writing in the *Contemporary Review* in 1873, perceived in Arthur's career 'the conflict continually maintained between the spirit and the flesh; and . . . the bearing down in history and in individual man of pure and lofty Christian purpose by the lusts of the flesh, by the corruptions of superstition, by human passions and selfishness'. Tennyson, for what it is worth, thought this one of the best accounts (*Memoir*, pp. 523–4). But the theme was no longer attractive by the time Ryals published his study in 1967. The effect of his version is to put a more general slant upon the *Idylls*, making them more acceptable to modern readers. Similarly, Ryals presents Arthur as 'a monomaniac . . . who would impose his values on the universe' (p. 81). This reading removes the need to take straightforwardly the moralizing in the poems, and it also relocates their interest in more fashionable existential notions of the self ('Arthur realizes himself by seeing his values projected into his knights', p. 81).

Second, Ryals asserts that his interpretation of the *Idylls* draws upon fundamental truths about humanity: in the passage I first quoted from his book he lays claim to 'all the contradictions of existence' (*all*?). Thus he procures authority both for the poems and his interpretation, and seems to render them significant for ever and hence for readers today. However, what he is promoting is actually a particular notion of the scope and potential of human lives. Despite the existentialist terminology, this is what might best be termed essentialist humanism. It propounds a quasi-spiritual idea of 'man', conceived as lonely but autonomous individual, poised between allegedly universal categories of experience; behind the idea is an attenuated Christianity.[5] All possibilities of meaning are, simultaneously, projected out onto a supposedly universal human condition and collapsed back into the individual consciousness. This perspective is found all the time in Tennyson criticism. It may seem vague and harmless enough, but it rules out effective consideration of the historical conditions which govern the activities of writing and reading (the poet's writing, the reading of successive generations). By removing from visibility the power structures and ideologies, the institutions and practices, which determine the conditions of actual lives, it inhibits political awareness and change.

Essentialist humanism lies behind even criticism which disclaims any interest in world views. Cleanth Brooks in *The Well Wrought Urn* (1947) insists that even if we can 'frame a proposition, a statement, which will adequately represent the total meaning of the poem', this is beside the point. What we should observe in a poem is 'a pattern of resolutions and balances and harmonizations, developed through a temporal scheme'.[6] This approach would seem to make relevance irrelevant, for whatever the poem is about, it may manifest paradoxes, ambiguities, ironies, tensions and resolutions of them. And so Brooks draws his examples from very different poets and historical periods. From Tennyson he takes 'Tears, Idle Tears', though he has to work rather hard to get the effect he prizes ('Are they *idle* tears? Or are they not rather the most meaningful of tears?' p. 136). However, at the very end of his book, Brooks comes clean and reveals the world view which underlies his formal preoccupations. The poet's 'task', he says, 'is finally to unify experience. He must return to us the unity of the experience itself as man knows it in his own experience' (p. 173). Brooks claims he is only responding to the poems, but he is actually prescribing a view of the world centred upon a coherent and autonomous entity, 'man', which is realized in the individual experiencing human subject. Between these two ('man' and the individual) there seems little space for social concerns or for the power structures which govern them. Indeed, Brooks works to make such matters seem insignificant, by using such exalted language as: 'Even after the worst has been said about man's multiple vision, the poet must somehow prove that the child is father to the man, that the dawn light is still somehow the same light as the evening light' (p. 174).

The political implications of Brooks' stance are evident

in his rejection of aspects of Tennyson's poetry which he finds unpromising for his kind of criticism. Tennyson, he says, grapples 'with the "big" questions which were up for his day', but this is of no value in the poetry, in Brooks' view, because Tennyson 'does not typically build them into the structure of the poetry itself as enriching ambiguities' (p. 136). Tennyson's engagement in issues which troubled his contemporaries is unhelpful, especially in so far as he took up positions which cannot be shown to be enriched – that is, undermined and rendered inert – by ambiguities.

The same mechanism is at work in the reluctance of critics to deal with Tennyson's hostility to the Oxford Movement and the growing influence of Roman Catholicism outside and inside the Church of England. Ryals acknowledges Tennyson's remark about the key significance of the mistaken asceticism of Percivale in 'The Holy Grail' – that it should be understood in terms of 'nineteenth-century temptations', evidently the Oxford Movement.[7] But Ryals sets aside this local and polemical reference and interprets Percivale as deluded 'about the possibilities of his own personality', and as 'an allegory of the poet's development' (pp. 171, 173). In essentialist humanism the crucial concepts are the individual consciousness and a realm of universal significance, into which one can be transported by special experiences like poetry. Purposeful involvement in political and social affairs is inappropriate.

For these critics, in almost so many words, Literature = the human condition = essentialist humanism (= relevance). The last term is in parentheses because such is the power of the formula that the question of relevance seems unnecessary: of course 'the human condition' is important. The formula makes Literature express a perspective from which, it appears, few could reasonably dissent. In the process it ensures, also, that few will ever be disturbed.

However, it is not sufficient to pose against the universal claims of the literary a demand for immediate personal relevance. This move is understandable: essentialist humanism defines literary texts as of quintessential 'human' significance, and the reader responds: 'All right, then it should speak directly to *me*.' The demand for 'relevance' comes to prominence in the 1960s. Already in 1964 Graham Hough observed that 'the ordinary English classics are no longer part of the natural formation of the young.'[8] Up to this point, it went *without saying* that the experience of reading Literature was important and good. 'Relevance' did not present itself as a question, because the young people who were being taught literary culture were so thoroughly immersed in it that it seemed, naturally, to speak to them. Hough himself grew up in a literary environment rather like Tennyson's. As a child he read a large part of the English classics simply as he found them around him; whereas lately it is 'quite common to find boys coming up for English scholarships who have not read any literature before 1900, beyond what they have had to read at school' (Hough, p. 104). Since that time, the reading of Literature from before 1900 (Shakespeare apart) has become far less common in schools. Cultural deference has helped to keep the institution going, but at the same time university and school students have developed an alternative culture of their own, producing, increasingly, the confidence to challenge established culture.[9] Hence the demand for 'relevance'. Led by academic criticism to expect an engagement with the 'human condition' and finding in fact some of the writing of certain class fractions in one corner of Europe during a few hundred years, readers ask at least that it should say something to them.

Relevance is an inadequate working principle because it requires too little of text and reader. Pressed to its logical conclusion, it asks merely that texts give back to readers their current concerns; it protects readers from the challenge of other perspectives and leaves them immured in their own preoccupations. And by asserting the primacy of the experiencing individual, it re-enacts a fundamental strategy of essentialist humanism: the individual (writer and reader) is imagined as the focus of meaning and truth.

But that is not how language and culture work. Actually, meaning is always dependent upon context: it is produced in history and ideology, within the prevailing power relations. Furthermore, by effacing difference, and the factors that determine it, the idea of relevance obscures the fact that things might be other than they are. This latter is a prerequisite for political change; and Literature, if we expect not universal truths but particular projects in particular historical conditions, can disturb and provoke us with attitudes illuminatingly different from our own.

A test case in Tennyson's writing is *Maud*. Modern literary intellectuals have generally been hostile to the idea, expressed at the end of the poem, that it is better for a nation to engage in wars overseas than to suffer 'the long, long canker of peace'.[10] Now, it is possible to argue the poem out of this implication, either by insisting that its dramatic construction absolves us from worry about the attitudes expressed; or, like Jerome H. Buckley, by excusing the speaker – suggesting that he 'knows nothing' of the Crimean War, that 'the ending of the false peace seems essential to the establishment of any true peace', that he is convinced only 'temporarily', and that 'the war is really a "moral equivalent" for the immoral war within'.[11] Thus the poem becomes superficially more acceptable – apparently more relevant and closer to what we might take to be universally true. But we lose the challenge which the poem otherwise offers – to share the experience of a speaker very different from ourselves, and so be provoked to understand why his position held substantial credibility for Tennyson and some of his contemporaries.

The final stanza, which Tennyson added to the poem in 1856 to cope with complaints about bellicosity, illustrates well the kind of sequence by which people argue themselves and others into killing:

Let it flame or fade, and the war roll down like a wind,
We have proved we have hearts in a cause, we are
noble still,

> And myself have awaked, as it seems, to the better
>   mind;
> It is better to fight for the good than to rail at the ill;
> I have felt with my native land, I am one with my
>   kind,
> I embrace the purpose of God, and the doom assigned.

The movement is from personal experience to generalizations about the nation as a whole (forgetting those already vilified for preferring peace); from there to humanity at large, 'my kind' (forgetting those belonging to the other side); and then to 'the purpose of God'. This is typical of the way ideology universalizes the perspective of a sectional interest. It may often be observed in justifications of war; and, indeed, in the self-justifications of essentialist-humanist literary criticism, as I have already presented them.

The present study does not seek to render Tennyson's poems coherent and agreeable, in the service of notions of the human condition or relevance. Rather, the text will be approached as initially Tennyson's project, devised within the current institutions and forms of writing, and producing a version of reality which it promotes as meaningful and persuasive at that historical conjuncture, in relation to the prevailing structures of power and ideology. Thus the text is envisaged, not as reflecting a historical situation in its totality, but as an interpretation and an intervention from a specific position in the social order. For although the dominant class or class fraction controls the terms and conditions within which writing is carried on, other classes and groups find ways to express and realize their particular positions and experiences, spaces in which to negotiate a relationship with the dominate ideology, even modes of resistance. The present study will seek to locate the text in its ideological field – the range of ideas and attitudes brought into play by the text; thereby distinguishing the preferred version of reality which constitutes the author's project, and laying open to investigation its complex and revealing relationships with social processes. The formal properties of the text will then appear as strategies which aim to make that preferred version vivid, coherent and persuasive. The text is opened up to understanding, and so to questioning.[12] This is not what is usually meant by 'relevance', but it may lead towards a positive engagement with the world.

Once it is in circulation, the text is also continuously reproduced – in changing times and places, including our own, for further purposes within developing institutions. We can have no innocent access to the text or to history. Hence the attention to the established modes of criticism in the present chapter: they construct 'the poems of Tennyson' for modern academic readers. Tennyson profoundly disliked all this. He disliked textual annotation ('many passages in Wordsworth and other poets had been entirely spoilt by the modern habit of giving every various reading along with the text'); and critical interpretation ('I hate to be tied down to say, "*This* means *that*", because the thought within the image is much more than any one interpretation'); and biographical enquiry ('my father often felt oppressed by the compliments and curiosity of undiscerning critics, and would say: "I hate the blare and blaze of so-called fame."')[13] Tennyson seems to have imagined that his writing could simply 'be itself', regardless of the contexts in which it is received. But this is a chimera: writing – all human behaviour – is always received in specific conditions, and interpreted as it is received. There is no free-floating realm of immediate communication between essential selves, writers or readers. The critics and institutions that have appropriated Tennyson's poetry are an inevitable part of the continuous process through which culture is produced. It is not because they have remade Tennyson that they may be criticized. It is because what they have made is politically regressive and because, as part of that politics, they efface their activity of making.

The present volume is of course a further production of Tennyson, part of the continuous production of culture; the foregoing chapter is, in part, an attempt to make space for my own work by clearing the ground, so to speak, of attitudes that impede it. And my work also is conceived and published in historical and political conditions. I cannot avoid the logic of Frank Lentricchia's argument that 'theories are generated only in history – no theory comes from outside – for the purpose of generating history in a certain way: generating the history we want'.[14] So I do not assert absolute epistemological superiority for my approach but, rather, these two claims: that the self-consciousness with which I acknowledge my own construction helps to avoid the (self) deception through which literary criticism commonly naturalizes its own stance; and that it is through politics in history that meanings can be contested and the world changed.

2 The Politics of Poetry

Poetry and Machinery

The dominant twentieth-century ideas about Literature would lead us to suppose that Tennyson's poetry would have relatively little to do with imperial expansion or electoral reform: those are matters for speeches rather than poems. Yeats has told us that out of the quarrel with others we make rhetoric, out of the quarrel with ourselves, poetry; Auden declared in a poem on the death of Yeats that 'poetry makes nothing happen.' The idea is fundamentally utilitarian; as I will show, it goes back to John Stuart Mill, who wrote: 'eloquence is heard, poetry is overheard.'[1]

But this is false in two senses. First, even poetry which appears to be remote from political issues is in fact involved with the political life of its society: it disseminates ideas, images and narratives of the way the world is, and that is always a political activity. It contributes to the way we understand ourselves and, as a relatively prestigious mode of cultural production, its influence may be considerable. Despite Yeats' disclaimer – indeed, partly because of it – many educated people in England get most of their idea of the Irish revolt of 1916 from Yeats' personalized view in 'Easter 1916'; and, along with that, the notion that the main issue was whether the leaders managed to transcend their despised (by Yeats) class origins and be heroic after all (though *paradoxically*, of course – straightforward admiration for violence not authorized by the state would not sit so easily on syllabuses). I will show that even Tennyson's poems which seem remote from the centres of power in his time are fully political in their implications.

Second, poetry had in Tennyson's time a directly political role. Wordsworth, Coleridge and Southey had welcomed the French Revolution and, despite their apostasy, this set the agenda for the political scope of poetry. In 1817, when Southey had become a government writer, radicals printed his *Wat Tyler* in a pirated edition to promote their cause. During the especially repressive period of the Napoleonic Wars and their aftermath, Byron, Shelley and Leigh Hunt opposed the government virulently in their writings, and Keats was associated with Hunt.

Tennyson's *Poems, Chiefly Lyrical* (1830) were received into a fully politicized literary scene. The largely hostile reviews of John Wilson ('Christopher North') and John Croker were from explicitly Tory journals, and they discerned in Tennyson a radical in the line of Shelley, Keats and Hunt. Wilson in *Blackwood's Edinburgh Magazine* enunciates an explicit conservative aesthetic: 'All human beings see the same light in heaven and in woman's eyes; and the great poets put it into language which rather records than reveals, spiritualizing while it embodies.'[2] There can be little reason for seeking any sudden improvement in society if all the great truths are already and inevitably there. Moreover all conflicts, potential or actual, are effaced by the claim that everyone has the same point of view. Wilson says, by way of example, that 'Scott, when eulogizing our love of our native land, uses the simplest language, and gives vent to the simplest feelings': translate them 'into any language, living or dead – and they will instantly be felt by all hearts, savage or civilized, to be the most exquisite poetry' (Armstrong, p. 109). The possibility of alternative relationships to one's country, for instance on the part of those who benefit least from its arrangements, is swept aside. This is felt to be proper: poetry has 'dominion over men, because of their common humanity' (p. 109). Wilson mistrusted what he saw as Tennyson's 'straining after originality – an aversion from the straightforward and strong simplicity of nature and truth' (p. 111), because it threatened to turn up something new and potentially subversive.

Wilson was disturbed also because there were few lines where Tennyson 'condescends to be patriotic' but yet he is 'a lover of liberty' (Armstrong, p. 110). The latter remark is perhaps made with tongue in cheek, for it refers to the little song 'The winds, as at their hour of birth', but it places Wilson nevertheless. His suspicion is that Tennyson tends towards the commitment to revolutionary change expressed by Shelley and other radicals. Shelley shared the idea that poetry plumbs universally valid emotions – it was almost unavoidable in the period. It grew during the eighteenth century as poetry became separated from an immediate relationship with the people for whom it was written. As poetry's potential public became remote and indefinite – anyone who could read – its claims became both more ambitious and more general.[3] But Shelley denied that the true values apprehended by the poet are those conventionally approved, and he did assert that ultimately they are made by people. He did this in *A Defence of Poetry* by invoking the origins of society: 'The social sympathies, or those laws from which as from its elements society results, begin to develop themselves from the moment that two human beings coexist.'[4] He declares that it is the poet's role to propagate these fundamental sympathies and laws, but they are not the commonplaces of the current system. They are 'equality, diversity, unity, contrast, mutual dependence' (*Defence*, pp. 24–5). Thus poetry, by definition, speaks the cause of political freedom, idealism is recruited in the service of equality and cooperation. The decay of poetry, Shelley asserts, accompanies social decay – as for instance in the reign of Charles II, when poems 'became hymns to the triumph of kingly power over liberty and virtue' (p. 38); and poets must move contemporary society 'into a subordination to the imaginative and creative faculty', producing in that effort the most memorable age in philosophical and poetic achievement since 'the last national struggle for civil and religious liberty' (p. 59).

What Shelley did, more fully than the young Wordsworth and more clearly than Blake, was align an exalted idea of poetic imagination with a noble idea of social justice, and he exemplified that conjunction in poems like 'Prometheus Unbound', 'The Mask of Anarchy', 'Ode to Liberty' and 'Ode to the West Wind'.[5] Freedom of the imagination correlates with political freedom.

Shelley's argument in the *Defence* is directed less against the traditional Toryism of Wilson than against the nexus of attitudes and theories through which the industrial revolution was being explained and promoted by manufacturers and intellectuals associated with them. In this he identified correctly the dominant movement of his time. He argued that utilitarianism, political economy and reliance upon machinery were destroying both imaginative and political freedom – they had advanced at the expense of the creative faculty, so that 'The rich have become richer, and the poor have become poorer' (*Defence*, p. 50).

The industrial revolution was giving the middle classes – manufacturers, traders, financiers and associated professionals – economic ascendancy over the landed aristocracy and gentry, and they sought political power and ideological hegemony also. 'Hegemony' is the term elaborated by Gramsci to address the way a class may achieve dominance in a particular socio-political situation, not so much by exercising manifest and direct control, but by gaining acceptance for its way of looking at the world: 'one concept of reality is diffused throughout society in all its institutional and private manifestations, informing with its spirit all taste, morality, customs, religious and political principles, and all social relations, particularly in their intellectual and moral connotation.'[6] Historians of diverse theoretical allegiances have shown that the middle classes secured during the nineteenth century just such a general acceptance for their way of looking at the world.[7] In the present chapter (concerned mainly with Tennyson's early work) I speak of a developing, later on of an established, bourgeois hegemony. (The facts that the landed aristocracy retained many key political positions, that it still owned most property, and that the middle classes deferred to it socially need not undermine this analysis.)

The 1832 Reform Act, which will be discussed in the next section, was the vehicle of the advancing political power of the middle classes. Utilitarianism, political economy and a belief in the virtues of machinery were crucial ideas in the development of their ideological hegemony. Political economists from Adam Smith, through David Ricardo and John Stuart Mill, assumed that humanity consists of sovereign individuals who pursue their self interest; and that when this self-interest is rightly discerned and allowed to work without check it produces a 'natural' social order (without the interference of vested interest, tradition or the like), and hence the most rapid increase in the 'wealth of nations' and hence in the happiness of all people. Through this ideology the traders, manufacturers and financiers claimed scientific justification for their practices, on the grounds that the unfettered operations of the market afforded the most efficient and natural way of producing wealth; and ethical justification because such wealth production would increase the happiness of everyone. The laws of the market would ensure rational distribution of the wealth and unfair and unreasonable restrictions would be abolished. These latter included restrictions on the franchise (so far as the middle classes were disqualified), laws against non-Anglicans (which manufacturers often were), the Corn Laws (which advantaged landed as against trading interests), and slavery (which diminished in importance as a source of wealth with the rise of manufacture).

It is important for us to realize the extent to which political economy and utilitarianism were dominated by ideas of machinery, for it helps to explain the opposition which Tennyson promulgated (and which still informs modern ideas of 'the arts') between transcendent kinds of truth and experience and the domains of politics, economics and everyday affairs. Charles Babbage in *On The Economy of Manufactures* (1832) was both typical and influential in his assertion that machinery was 'contributing to the improvement, the wealth, and the happiness of our race'; in fact, it was in collaboration with the natural:

> Whether he employs the regulated action of steam, or the more tremendous effects of gunpowder, he is only producing on a small scale compositions and decompositions which nature is incessantly at work in reversing, for the restoration of that equilibrium which we cannot doubt is constantly maintained throughout even the remotest limits of our systems.[8]

Marx and Engels were to remark 'the selfish misconception that induces you [the bourgeoisie] to transform into eternal laws of nature and of reason the social forms springing from your present mode of production and form of property'.[9] Babbage was Professor of Mathematics at Cambridge when Tennyson was there; later on he wrote to Tennyson about the lines 'Every minute dies a man, / Every minute one is born' ('A Vision of Sin'), suggesting that this 'erroneous calculation . . . should be corrected as follows: "Every minute dies a man / And one and a sixteenth is born".' Tennyson compromised with this statistical imperative and changed 'minute' in each line to 'moment'.[10]

Politics also was seen in terms of machinery: for instance, Joseph Hume warmed Parliament that if it 'did not represent all classes, it became a bad engine – an engine in the hands of the few'. So was ethics: Andrew Ure explained in *The Philosophy of Manufactures* that it is 'excessively the interest of every mill-owner, to organize his moral machinery on equally sound principles with his mechanical'.[11] The insistent use of this image prompted Carlyle's opposition between the Dynamical and Mechanical natures of 'Man', and Shelley's sense that 'the mechanical arts' were opposed to 'the creative faculty'. And hence Macaulay's belief that 'as civilization advances, poetry almost necessarily declines': political economy has improved since Walpole and mathematics since Newton, 'But language, the machine of the poet, is best fitted for his purpose in its rudest state.' A poetry/science dichotomy was fundamental to the literary theory of John Stuart Mill.[12]

Utilitarians developed three ways of handling poetry: relegation, incorporation and marginalization. Many were inclined, simply, to dismiss it as frivolous. One said in the *Westminster Review*, a utilitarian organ, that he would be 'glad to be informed, how the universal pursuit of literature and poetry, poetry and literature, is to conduce towards cotton spinning'.[13] Babbage in *The Economy of Manufactures* declared: 'science has called into real existence the visions of the poet' (p. 319). This position became established as one of the ways of thinking about poetry and we still have it today: it is all very well, but not much use to anyone (try telling people you are writing a book on Tennyson). Poetry is *relegated*.

A more sophisticated utilitarianism sought to incorporate poetry, and this is the project of William Johnson Fox's review of *Poems, Chiefly Lyrical* in the *Westminster Review*. Fox begins by associating poetry directly with the advance in manufacturing processes:

> It would be a pity that poetry should be an exception to the great law of progression that obtains in human affairs; and it is not. The machinery of a poem is not less susceptible of improvement than the machinery of a cotton-mill; nor is there any better reason why the one should retrograde from the days of Milton, than the other from those of Arkwright. (Armstrong, p. 71)

Poetry can be part of the forward march of humanity because of its own particular utility. Fox suggests two main ways in which this may happen. One, with which he concludes, is that poets can arouse good attitudes in the people:

They can influence the associations of unnumbered minds; they can command the sympathies of unnumbered hearts; they can disseminate principles; they can give those principles power over men's imaginations; they can excite in a good cause the sustained enthusiasm that is sure to conquer; they can blast the laurels of the tyrants, and hallow the memories of the martyrs of patriotism; they can act with a force, the extent of which it is difficult to estimate, upon national feelings and character, and consequently upon national happiness. (Armstrong, p. 83)

This is in a way not unlike Shelley, and Fox relates it to Tennyson by quoting from his Shelleyan poem 'The Poet'. But it is even more like Wilson, in that the principles the poet is supposed to disseminate are not those of equality and cooperation but those of the developing bourgeois hegemony. This is apparent in Fox's emphasis on patriotism (we can be sure that the 'tyrants' are foreign) and 'happiness', together with his overriding definition of 'progression' as exemplified in 'the machinery of a cotton-mill'. He was seeking to achieve full hegemony for the manufacturers, financiers and traders to whom utilitarianism appealed; he did not want poets combining imaginative and political freedom into a powerful agent of political change. He wanted poetry *incorporated* into bourgeois ideology (compare Mill's comment on Monckton Milnes' 'Lay of the Humble': it goes straight to the heart of humanity'[14]).

Incorporation was for utilitarianism an alternative to relegation as a way of handling poetry. A third possibility partakes of both, and in its terms Fox framed almost all of his appreciation of Tennyson – it seemed to him the point at which poetry could progress. The idea is that poetry should concentrate on 'the analysis of particular states of mind' (Armstrong, p. 75). 'Supposed Confessions' is an instance: 'Such topics are more in accordance with the spirit and intellect of the age than those about which poetry has been accustomed to be conversant; their adoption will effectually redeem it from the reproach of being frivolous and enervating' (p. 77). Fox admires also 'The Merman', 'Mariana' and 'A spirit haunts the year's last hours': Tennyson 'can cast his own spirit into any living thing, real or imaginary' (p. 77). This may seem a good recipe for poetry, but that is because we are still within the utilitarian frame of thinking (as I will show later in the chapter). In the context of Fox's argument, it can be seen that what is being offered to poetry is the space which is left when the main business of the world has been done elsewhere. Shelley's claim to address the most important human issues – the way a whole society functions – is disallowed: imaginative freedom and political freedom are split apart, and to poetry is left 'states of mind'. This strategy resembles both relegation and incorporation, but it is nevertheless distinct: poetry is a valued part of the utilitarian world so long as it does not intrude on the real conditions of life. It is *marginalized*.

Arthur Hallam's review of *Poems, Chiefly Lyrical* takes a further step: it disputes the assumption of Wilson and Fox alike, that poetry can and should deal in values of general relevance. Hallam denies that the best poems are the 'most universally agreeable, which take for their primary subject the *usual* passions of the heart, and deal with them in a simple state' (Armstrong, p. 90). This may have been possible in the time of Shakespeare, Hallam thinks, but since then there has been a 'change in the relative position of artists to the rest of the community' and therefore 'modern poetry, in proportion to its depth and truth, is likely to have little immediate authority over public opinion' (p. 92). This argument is of the utmost import-ance: it signals the beginning of a self-conscious avant-garde – already implicit in the career of Keats but subject to his anxiety about the agony of human hearts. Keats, still, felt that the poet should be central in the awareness of his society; Hallam argues that this cannot, indeed should not, be so because (taking up Fox's second position) poets like Keats, Shelley and Tennyson are so far ahead of other people in their states of mind:

> How should they be popular, whose senses told them a richer and ampler tale than most men could understand, and who constantly expressed, because they constantly felt, sentiments of exquisite pleasure or pain, which most men were not permitted to experience? The public very naturally derided them as visionaries. (Armstrong, p. 88)

Hallam denies that distinctively modern poetry has anything to do with general principles at all: Keats, Shelley and Tennyson are 'poets of sensation rather than reflection. Susceptible of the slightest impulse from external nature, their fine organs trembled into emotions at colours, and sounds, and movements, unperceived or unregarded by duller temperaments' (p. 87). Notice how Shelley's scope is limited by the term 'poet of sensation'. As Patrick Parrinder observes, he 'came to personify the charisma and magic of poethood for generations of Victorians who had no time for his political views'.[15]

Hallam appears to desire an autonomous role for poetry, as a visionary field of exquisite sensations where the poet's authority is unique. But this idea colludes with the utilitarian extraction of the poet from the rest of human affairs and from politics in particular. Hallam actually offers as Tennyson's 'advantage' over Keats and Shelley the fact 'that he comes before the public unconnected with any political party, or peculiar system of opinions' (Armstrong, pp. 92–3). So Hallam separates himself explicitly from the thought, 'urged in some of our fashionable publications, that the diffusion of poetry must necessarily be in the direct ratio of the diffusion of machinery'. He does not want poetry associated with the ideology of manufacture: he believes that 'Art herself, less manifestly glorious than in her periods of undisputed supremacy, retains her essential prerogatives' (p. 92). Yet his position is shaped in response to utilitarianism.

Hallam stands at the beginning of a movement which has sought to privilege poetry by claiming for it a status far beyond ordinary human experience, but has succeeded only in quarantining it from the main concerns of economic and political life. The main institutions of poetry have long adopted as their only real alternatives incorporation into the dominant ethos and marginalization as an avant-garde specialism. Most people, of course, hardly think of poetry at all: for them it is relegated. Tennyson experienced divergent demands: to incorporate his writing into the cultural apparatus of the developing bourgeois state, and to work in a special, marginal region which would not interfere with the real business of making money and securing bourgeois hegemony.

Freedom and the Bourgeoisie

Tennyson's relationship with the ideology of manufacture was always ambivalent. As the third son of a rural parson, his allegiance lay in the countryside, with the traditional, conservative gentry, stratified by wealth and status in terms of the ownership of land. But his relationship with this system was complicated hugely by a resentment of his grandfather and uncle. The former had disinherited Tennyson's unstable father, depriving the family of money and standing which might have been theirs. At the same time, the grandfather's mode of increasing his wealth (by devious buying and selling of land) and the uncle's grandiose pretensions rendered them highly vulnerable to the scorn of Tennyson and his immediate family (Martin, *Tennyson*, pp. 3–9, 205–9). Resentment at the arrogant manners and peremptory power of those who dominated in the traditional hierarchy of social relations surfaces continually in Tennyson's poems (in 'Lady Clara Vere de Vere', 'Locksley Hall', *The Princess, Maud*). The obvious alternative was an identification with bourgeois progressivism, and in part this is how we think of Tennyson. The closing lines of *In Memoriam* envisage the future:

> Of those that, eye to eye, shall look
>> On knowledge; under whose command
>> Is Earth and Earth's, and in their hand
> Is Nature like an open book.

This is the ideal self-image of political economy. But elsewhere, for instance in *In Memoriam* 114, Tennyson derogates 'knowledge' in relation to 'wisdom' and 'reverence'. In so doing, he holds to a notion of conservative, intuitive understanding, rooted inevitably in a traditional social order. Lady Clara Vere de Vere is blamed for enticing and rejecting a young yeoman to feed her pride. She is told that 'Kind hearts are more than coronets', but the conclusion of the poem validates the traditional social role of the gentry:

> If time be heavy on your hands,
> Are there no beggars at your gate,
>> Nor any poor about your lands?

No doubt there were, and Tennyson appeals to ideal notions of the established order to deal with them, not to the progress to be expected from political economy. It is from within this complex personal feeling about the English class structure that Tennyson began to negotiate the growing power of the ideology of manufacture.

The year 1830, when Tennyson published *Poems, Chiefly Lyrical*, and the two years that followed, saw revolutionary movements in many European countries and major upheavals in England. Tennyson took up the suggestion that he might concentrate on states of mind, and began writing 'Oenone', 'The Lotos-Eaters', 'Ulysses', 'Tithonus' and *In Memoriam* (though these poems *are* in fact shot through with political issues). But he also attempted to work out an explicit political position in a series of poems written in 1831–3. He did not sing of the principles which could make people happy while they spun cotton; but he did investigate what could be said for bourgeois ideology in the wake of the Shelleyan mode.

Harold Bloom has argued that every poet

> is in the position of being 'after the Event', in terms of literary language. His art is necessarily an *aftering*, and so at best he strives for a selection, through repression, out of the traces of the language of poetry: that is, he represses some of the traces, and remembers others.[16]

Bloom's awareness that poems are 'words that refer to other words, and *those* words refer to still other words, and so on, into the densely overpopulated world of literary language' (*Poetry and Repression*, p. 3) is valuable. However, Bloom limits his theory to the discourses of poetry, and in Tennyson's case, perhaps because his psychoanalytical model works better like that, he identifies just one precursor poet with whom Tennyson is struggling: Keats. Bloom's concern is with Tennyson's need, which he must repress, to transform and triumph over the inevitable influence of Keats; the guilt and anxiety in Tennyson's poems is interpreted as manifesting this need and repression.

Bloom's theory, then, isolates Tennyson from the other discourses in which he was inserted. But even within literary history it is false to see Tennyson as having only Keats to cope with as a model. In particular, he said in 1869: 'Nobody admires Shelley more than I once did' (*Memoir*, p. 475); and Shelley was the poet most in vogue at Cambridge when Tennyson was there in the late 1820s.[17] As I have argued, Shelley insisted on conjoining political and imaginative freedom, and Tennyson wrote a sonnet 'To Poesy' in this vein in 1828:

> Methinks I see the world's renewed youth
>   A long day's dawn, when Poesy shall bind
> Falsehood beneath the altar of great Truth:
> The clouds are sundered towards the morning-rise;
>   Slumber not now, gird up thy loins for fight,
> And get thee forth to conquer.

This sonnet, which begins 'O God, make this age great', is not very clear about its political principles, but it has the manner of Shelley's 'Ode to Liberty' (published 1820) – of this, for instance:

> The eager hours and unreluctant years
>   As on a dawn-illumined mountain stood,
> Trampling to silence their loud hopes and fears,
>   Darkening each other with their multitude,
> And cried aloud, 'Liberty!'[18]

The manner appears in *Poems, Chiefly Lyrical* in 'The Poet':

> And Freedom reared in that august sunrise
>   Her beautiful bold brow,
> When rites and forms before his [i.e. the poet's]
>   burning eyes
>   Melted like snow.

Much more insistently than Shelley (cf. 'Ode to Liberty' stanzas 12 and 18), Tennyson links freedom to non-violence and wisdom, and this no doubt helped Fox to accept the poem as an account of the incorporated poet (Armstrong, p. 83). Tennyson is already engaged in renegotiating Shelley's link between poetic inspiration and freedom. He retains the visionary mode of Romanticism, but with diminished political content.

It must be admitted that the writing in 'Ode to Liberty', although that poem is rooted in a specific issue (an uprising in Spain), lends itself to appropriation in the service of a vaguer idea of freedom than Shelley actually held. Indeed, Tennyson's sense of the Shelleyan position was, no doubt, mediated already through the depoliticizing reworking of the Cambridge 'apostle' F. D. Maurice. In a series of 'Sketches of Contemporary Authors', published in the *Athenaeum* in 1828, Maurice attributes to Shelley the most exalted idea of poetic imagination ('he divides the light from the darkness, and pours the one into a focus of unmingled love, wherein his thoughts disport like birds in the radiance of the setting sun, and piles the other into a black and beamless chaos, thronged through all its desolate immensity with blind, imperfect shapes of terror and hatred'.[19]) But Maurice's main effort is to discount Shelley's opinions – explaining that 'those of his notions which seem, at first sight, the most awfully mischievous, are frequently erroneous in shape rather than in matter, in expression rather than in idea' (pp. 72–3). He presents a Shelley imbued with general moral conviction but subject to 'a hot and rushing impetuosity' (p. 71).

Actually, Shelley could be very specific about freedom, as he was in 'The Mask of Anarchy' which he wrote after the Peterloo Massacre in 1819, when yeomanry wielding sabres attacked 80,000 unarmed people trapped in a small space and killed eleven of them, including a child. 'What is Freedom?', the poem asks, and the reply is precise enough:

> For the labourer thou art bread,
> And a comely table spread
> From his daily labour come
> In a neat and happy home.

> Thou art clothes, and fire, and food
> For the trampled multitude –
> No – in countries that are free
> Such starvation cannot be
> As in England now we see.

(stanzas 54, 55)

Shelley has a specific proposal: that people assemble in such numbers that their assailants will finally be daunted by the extent of the killing required:

> With folded arms and steady eyes,
> And little fear, and less surprise,
> Look upon them as they slay
> Till their rage has died away.

> Then they will return with shame
> To the place from which they came,
> And the blood thus shed will speak
> In hot blushes on their cheek.

(stanzas 85, 86)

And then the nation will be inspired to rise – it is a credible political strategy –

> Rise like Lions after slumber
> In unvanquishable number –
> Shake your chains to earth like dew
> Which in sleep had fallen on you –
> Ye are many – they are few.

(stanza 91)

This stanza became a rallying call for the British labour movement.

'The Mask of Anarchy' was not published until 1832, but that was just the moment when Tennyson was working out in verse what he understood by freedom. Moreover, the publisher was Edward Moxon, who was the proprietor of the *Englishman's Magazine* in which Hallam's review of *Poems, Chiefly Lyrical* was printed, and who had already agreed to publish Tennyson's 1833 volume of poems (actually December 1832).[20] Tennyson could hardly ignore the Shelleyan conjunction of imaginative and political freedom. At another point in history (with Tory repression slightly alleviated and the impetus towards bourgeois hegemony much increased), coming from another class and being of a quite different temperament, Tennyson had to forge a new relationship between poetry and politics. The structure of attitudes which I have derived from utilitarianism allowed for the imaginative power of poetry so long as it kept clear of controversial political and economic issues – either by accepting the marginal role of exploring states of mind, or by enunciating general principles conducive to popular happiness. Within this latter alternative a Shelleyan invocation of freedom might be acceptable provided that it was vague, non-violent and concerned with the freedom of the middle class. Fundamentally, the Shelleyan correlation of imaginative and political freedom was split apart; Tennyson had more substantial issues to be anxious about than Harold Bloom allows. The poems of 1831–3 attempt a range of more and less satisfactory resolutions.

It is always easier to admire revolutions when they are other people's. But Tennyson and his Cambridge friends were actively involved in the Spanish revolt of 1830, inspired in part perhaps by Shelley's 'Ode to Liberty'; Tennyson and Hallam travelled through France to take money to the conspirators. The revolt was quickly and bloodily suppressed. The main impact on Tennyson seems to have been something which happened with Arthur Hallam in the valley of Cauteretz ('Recurrently sounding through the poetry written after the Pyrenean trip is the word "valley", always connected with love, usually with youth, and frequently with Arthur Hallam').[21] The Polish revolution of 1830–1 was far more sustained, and Tennyson wrote two sonnets, one urging the Poles to 'Break through your iron shackles', and other lamenting their suppression by the Russian Czar – 'that o'er grown Barbarian in the East'. The language and sentiments are Shelley's in, for instance, the sonnet 'Feelings of a Republican on the Fall of Bonaparte'. (There was general Russophobia in Britain in the 1830s;[22] the Czar was to recur in Tennyson's work as the figure of a tyrant who could be safely contrasted with the English government).

'Of old sat Freedom on the heights' is far less confident in its stance. It seems to begin with the Shelleyan vision:

Of old sat Freedom on the heights,
   The thunders breaking at her feet:
Above her shook the starry lights:
   She heard the torrents meet.

There in her place she did rejoice,
   Self-gathered in her prophet-mind,
But fragments of her mighty voice
   Came rolling on the wind.

Freedom, it seems, was for a long time remote and heard of only in 'fragments'. Then she moved in closer, but as this happens she is deprived of her prophetic mode and is revealed only 'part by part':

Then stept she down through town and field
　　To mingle with the human race,
And part by part to men revealed
　　The fulness of her face.

Probably Tennyson is thinking of certain phases of the seventeenth-century English revolution; elsewhere he gives special attention to the parliamentary leader John Hampden, whom he seems to have associated with Hallam. But freedom is certainly becoming more oblique in this stanza, and as Tennyson goes on the poem becomes scarcely coherent (Sir Charles Tennyson speaks of 'compressed and not always easily interpreted aphorisms')[23]:

Grave mother of majestic works,
　　From her isle-altar gazing down,
Who, God-like, grasps the triple forks,
　　And, King-like, wears the crown:

Her open eyes desire the truth.
　　The wisdom of a thousand years
Is in them.

The 'triple forks', Tennyson explained, are reminiscent of Zeus with his thunderbolts. The use of images of majesty, priesthood, deity and monarchy utterly reverses the Shelleyan treatment of freedom by associating it with all those forces which it was customarily supposed to overthrow. That Tennyson did not share liberal and egalitarian aspirations we may understand; but what he thought freedom was *from*, if not majesty, priesthood, deity and monarchy, is not readily apparent. He appeals instead to 'The wisdom of a thousand years'. Nor is it easy to see where freedom is, for in the previous stanza she had stepped down to mingle with the human race whereas now she seems to be back on the heights, or anyway on 'her isle-altar gazing down'. The clouds clear at the end of the poem:

May perpetual youth
Keep dry their light from tears;

That her fair form may stand and shine,
  Make bright our days and light our dreams,
Turning to scorn with lips divine
  The falsehood of extremes!

Freedom is remote again, an image to 'stand and shine', a
feature of dreams, not something to be acted upon. Yet
there is some impetus here, for freedom has scorn – for 'The
falsehood of extremes!' (thunderbolts, it seems, are not
extreme). It is urgency and energy of change that actually
disturbs Tennyson, and the role of freedom is to restrain it;
then the poem clarifies. This movement, from a potentially
Shelleyan exaltation of freedom to a conservative anxiety
about extremes, is acknowledged, with amusing precision,
in Wordsworth's response when the poem was read to him
in 1842. He 'listened with a gradually deepening attention'
and finally pronounced it to be 'very solid and noble in
thought' (*Memoir*, p. 175).

The extremes and the freedoms Tennyson was seeking to
negotiate were not just matters of poetic theory. In 1830
agricultural labourers across the south of England, whose
destitution and degradation had been amply catalogued by
Cobbett, broke threshing machines and machinery in iron
foundries and paper mills. They did not appreciate the
political economists' argument for machinery; as William
Carpenter pointed out, capitalists received the profits from
machines, whereas 'the labourer, being familiar only with
the amazing power of machinery in superseding his labour,
which is *the only commodity* he has to offer in exchange for the
necessary articles of subsistence, contends that machinery
necessarily produces poverty, and ought therefore to be
suppressed or destroyed.'[24] A landowner near Canterbury
calculated that a threshing machine in his parish would
take the occupations of fifteen men who might be assumed
to have sixty dependents.[25] In Wiltshire, where disorders
were repressed especially severely, Mr Justice Alderson
harangued the labourers he was sentencing about threshing
machines: 'If they are profitable to the farmer, they will

also be profitable ultimately to the labourer, though they may for a time injure him.'[26] But the starving people could not wait for the 'ultimate' profit. Babbage was at least more realistic than this: he debated soberly with himself whether it were better that workers 'should be at once driven out of trade by [machinery]; or whether it is more advantageous for them to be gradually forced to quit the trade'. He thought the former, and recommended friendly societies and 'a diversity of employments among members of the one family' as ways of handling the problem.[27]

Tennyson was at Cambridge during the labourers' revolt, and he helped to put out fires and 'paraded, armed with stout clubs' to defend the town – which was not in fact attacked;[28] at the same time, he 'largely sympathized with the labourers in their demands' (*Memoir*, p. 35). He wrote fifty years later in 'To Mary Boyle' that 'lowly minds were maddened to the height/By tonguester tricks'. He used the image of burning ricks in *The Princess* to evoke Ida's angry countenance:

> As of some fire against a stormy cloud,
> When the wild peasant rights himself, the rick
> Flames, and his anger reddens in the heavens.
>
> (IV, 365–7)

In all, 1,976 prisoners were tried in connection with the disturbances; 19 of them were judicially killed and 481 were transported.[29] The 'wild peasant' did not succeed in righting himself; in 1834 the Tolpuddle Martyrs were transported for trying to form an agricultural workers' union. A recurrent theme in Tennyson's political poems of 1831–3 is the danger of civil disturbance – 'A noise of hands that disarrange/The social engine', he calls it in 'Hail Briton!', adopting the mechanistic imagery. This is what he feared and what he meant above all by 'The falsehood of extremes'.

The Parliamentary Reform Bill of 1832 was conceived substantially in response to agrarian and industrial unrest. The idea was not to extend the franchise to those who might revolt, but to draw the manufacturing and trading interest into alliance with the landed aristocracy against the workers. 'It is of the utmost importance', Lord Grey said, 'to associate the middle with the higher orders of society in the love and support of the institutions and government of the country'.[30] The illegal newspaper *The Poor Man's Guardian* (illegal because it sold for 1d, not paying the government tax of 4d) warned the lower classes against supporting the bill:

> This on the face of the measure appears, at first sight, a most liberal alteration. What! extend the number of voters from one hundred and fifty thousand, to six or seven hundred thousand? *Most liberal indeed*!!! . . . those whose influence is already tenfold too great, are to have that influence tenfold increased, while you whose influence is already tenfold too little, are to have that influence (through the great increase of the other) incalculably diminished, it is the most *illiberal*, the most *tyrannical*, the most *abominable* . . .[31]

Nevertheless, many working people were deceived into believing that the reform would be in their interest, and in the comings and goings before it was passed their demonstrations were a major factor. The whole sequence was very messy: a general election returned many zealous reformers and the bill was passed but thrown out by the House of Lords; there were mass disturbances in London; the Commons passed the bill again but the Lords and the King still refused to accept it; the government resigned and, amid further popular demonstrations, the Duke of Wellington tried and failed to form an anti-reform administration. E. P. Thompson judges that 'Britain was within an ace of revolution.' Certainly contemporaries thought so: Francis Place wrote, 'We were within a moment of general rebellion, and had it been possible for the Duke of Wellington to have formed an administration the Thing [i.e. the establishment] and the people would have been at issue.'[32] Faced with this threat, the King and the Lords finally backed down.

It was in this context that Tennyson tried to redefine the Shelleyan watchword 'freedom', and it drove him into a commitment to the dominant middle-class order. He managed to reconstruct the Reform Bill combination of reaction, self-interest, progress and coercion in terms of a Whig view of history, even as it was happening. In 'I loving Freedom for herself' he presents two alternative paths for the British constitution: one is all dignified, purposeful, peaceful and passes the Reform Bill, the other is entirely disastrous and concludes with some unspecified 'shame':

> What nobler than an ancient land
>   That passing an august decree
> Makes wider in a settled peace
>   The lists of liberty?
>
> What baser than a land that falls
>   From freedom crying on her name
> Through cycles of disastrous change
>   To forge the links of shame?
>
> (lines 25–32)

The popular discontent which contributed so powerfully to reform is separated off and the Shelleyan vision is deprived of impetus; in fact, it seems that there is little to be envisioned, for 'The state within herself concludes/The power to change' (17–18) and the whole sequence proves that 'There lives a power to shape our ends/Rough-hew them as we will!' (55–6). Freedom is reworked as that which the bourgeoisie can secure for itself allegedly without breaching the peace, and events are handled so as to make it seem that this is what is being achieved. Tennyson here commits himself to a definition of freedom as that which frees the bourgeoisie, and refuses the rights of everyone else. I shall call it 'bourgeois freedom'. The underlying assumption is perhaps Macaulay's:

> The higher and middling orders are the natural representatives of the human race. Their interest may be opposed, in some things, to that of their proper

contemporaries, but it is identical with that of the innumerable generations which are to follow.[33]

That Tennyson was not unaware of the contradictions in his project may be inferred from another poem written at the same time, published in 1872 as 'England and America in 1782'. It was commonplace amongst radicals to invoke the American Revolution as a precedent: as Chartism grew the slogan 'No taxation without representation' was much used and the case for armed revolt was made – for instance by Peter Bussey at Hartshead Moor in 1838:

> What was it gained the independence of America? It was common sense and American Rifles. (*Loud cheering*.) If ever the people of England mean to obtain their independence, if ever they calculated upon uprooting the tyranny which now depresses their industry, they too will have to provide themselves with rifles. (*Cheers, and 'We will'*)[34]

Tennyson handles the American Revolution so as to identify it with the tendency in England to institute bourgeois freedom, rather than with any lower-class upheaval (he is addressing the English):

> What wonder, if in noble heat
> Those men thine arms withstood,
> Retaught the lesson thou hadst taught,
> And in thy spirit with thee fought –
> Who sprang from English blood!

The Americans were bourgeois English really, defending English ideals of freedom which had slipped temporarily since the seventeenth-century example of Hampden.

The anti-slavery movement, about which Tennyson was enthusiastic, was also open to distressing analogies with the home front. Richard Oastler made a typical comment in the *Leeds Mercury* in 1830:

> The very streets which receive the droppings of an 'Anti-Slavery Society' are every morning wet by the

tears of innocent victims at the accursed shrine of avarice, who are *compelled* (not by the cart-whip of the negro slave-driver) but by the dread of the equally appalling thong or strap of the over-looker, to hasten, half-dressed, *but not half-fed*, to those magazines of British infantile slavery – *the worsted mills in the town and neighbourhood of Bradford!!!*[35]

The British abolished slavery in the West Indies in 1834. The reasons were economic as well as humanitarian: Adam Smith had pointed out that it was extremely inefficient; and anyway English trade now depended on cotton manufacture rather than sugar and slaves.[36] Tennyson in 'O Mother Britain lift thou up' found reason only for British self-congratulation, even suggesting that the West Indies had been acquired *in order* to free slaves:

O let the far-off shores be glad,
    The isles break out in song,
For thou didst buy them with a price
    To ransom them from wrong.

The dismantling of the Shelleyan ideal of imaginative and political freedom had implications also for the role of the poet. For Shelley, he or she was necessarily in the vanguard of progress, and poetic rapture and political vision coincided. So in 'Ode to Liberty', in the first stanza, liberty gleams again in Spain, 'Scattering contagious fire into the sky', and poetry takes off in consequence:

My soul spurned the chains of its dismay,
    And in the rapid plumes of song
    Clothed itself, sublime and strong
(As a young eagle soars the morning clouds among),
    Hovering in verse o'er its accustomed prey:
    Till from its station in the Heaven of fame
    The Spirit's whirlwind rapped it . . .

Tennyson's adoption of a more cautious politics involves also a more cautious poetic: he begins,

I loving Freedom for herself,
   And much of that which is her form,
Wed to no faction in the state,
   A voice before the storm –

I mourn in spirit, when I think
   The year that comes may come with shame . . .

The poet stands outside faction but hardly above it – to one side, rather. He is tentative (for instance in line 2), able only to react. The fourth line keeps alive the possibility that he can prophesy like Cassandra, but it may mean, also, that he is driven before the storm – the mourning spirit suggests the more passive role. Either way, there is no sense that the poet's voice can *ride with* the storm: confidence in imaginative freedom collapses with confidence in political freedom. The lines are fluent enough, but they embody no implication, such as Shelley states in his image of the young eagle 'Hovering in verse o'er its accustomed prey', that poetic language might assert a privileged political insight.

Tennyson's poetic role has been constructed problematically: he is invited to disseminate lofty principles but only those which are compatible with bourgeois freedom. He struggles to readjust the Shelleyan watchword 'freedom' to those demands, but his writing barely masks the political realities underlying middle-class society and he fails to sustain a language assertive of imaginative freedom.

Tennyson's awareness of the position into which he had been manoeuvred, and especially of the constraints it imposed upon an ideal of imaginative freedom, is apparent in the most important poem of this group, 'You ask me, why, though ill at ease'. He makes the case now for a distinctively bourgeois freedom: it is not on the heights with starry lights and so on, but 'sober-suited' and 'slowly broadens down'. Nevertheless, he is 'ill at ease' and professes another commitment: his spirits 'languish for the purple seas'. If English freedom proved disappointing he would be all too ready to 'seek a warmer sky . . . The palms and temples of the South'. Imaginative and political freedom diverge.

You ask me, why, though ill at ease,
   Within this region I subsist,
   Whose spirits falter in the mist,
And languish for the purple seas.

It is the land that freemen till,
   That sober-suited Freedom chose,
   The land, where girt with friends or foes
A man may speak the thing he will;

A land of settled government,
   A land of just and old renown,
   Where Freedom slowly broadens down
From precedent to precedent:

Where faction seldom gathers head,
   But by degrees to fulness wrought,
   The strength of some diffusive thought
Hath time and space to work and spread.

Should banded unions persecute
   Opinion, and induce a time
   When single thought is civil crime,
And individual freedom mute;

Though Power should make from land to land
   The name of Britain trebly great –
   Though every channel of the State
Should fill and choke with golden sand –

Yet waft me from the harbour-mouth,
   Wild wind! I seek a warmer sky,
   And I will see before I die
The palms and temples of the South.

Looked at in the context of other discourses of the time, Tennyson's account seems almost set up to provoke dispute – as if he is manifestly overstating his case to set up the desirability of 'The palms and temples of the South'. 'It is the land that freemen till': yes indeed, but the introduction of bourgeois economic relations into the countryside –

turning land into a commodity and placing it in the hands of men willing to develop its productive resources for the market, and turning the rural population into freely mobile wage-workers – was betraying the vast majority of the free tillers into the severest economic bondage. Eric Hobsbawm explains:

> The classical British solution produced a country in which perhaps 4,000 proprietors owned perhaps four-sevenths of the land which was cultivated – I take the 1851 figures – by a quarter of a million farmers (three-quarters of the acreage being in farms of from 50 to 500 acres) who employed about one and a quarter million of hired labourers or servants.[37]

Continuity of employment had been destroyed by the increasing use of short contracts, even weekly or daily, the social gulf between farmer and labourer widened, wages were cut to below subsistence level, and people pauperized and driven into industrial towns by the poor laws.

The claim that 'A man may speak the thing he will' is equally extraordinary. At the time when the poem was written, a bitter campaign was being waged against the fourpenny government stamp on newspapers, which had been imposed following Peterloo in an attempt to place the dissemination of ideas beyond the pockets of working people. Those who published and sold papers like the *Poor Man's Guardian* were severely punished: some were flogged, and up to a thousand were imprisoned, including women with their babies. The publisher of the *Voice of the West Riding* told the magistrates in 1833: 'The object of the paper was to teach the productive classes the means by which they might extricate themselves from their degraded state of thraldom, and place society upon a basis where every individual member of the social brotherhood should enjoy his just rights and no more.'[38] But that was not allowed to be written and read, or not unless you had money. In so far as relative press freedom was obtained – and the immediate result of the reduction in stamp duty in 1836 was that the radical press was destroyed because it was no longer worth risking untaxed publication at 1d and the poor could not pay more – it was the outcome of bitter struggles by working people, not of a freedom broadening down from precedent to precedent.

Challenging such injustices is also disallowed; bourgeois freedom doesn't extent that far. Tennyson's poem opposes 'banded unions' to 'individual freedom' as if this were a necessary opposition, whereas those in the union movement actually intended to gain for their members, by the only means available to them, the freedoms which upper class individuals already enjoyed. Marx and Engels were to comment in the *Communist Manifesto*: 'by "individual" you mean no other person than the bourgeois, than the middle-class owner of property.'[39]

What is so crucial in this poem is Tennyson's admission that, despite his attempt to make a case for bourgeois freedom, his spirits languish for the purple seas. He acknowledges a divided allegiance. Politically bourgeois freedom is good but imaginatively he craves for something else. In effect, Tennyson is tempted to accept the marginalized rather than the incorporated role by indulging in an imaginative engagement with remote places. Ironically, we can discern two kinds of marginalized person in the poem: the poet, whose imaginative freedom is only partially respected within the developing bourgeois hegemony; and the lower classes, who are excluded from bourgeois freedom even by Tennyson himself (not being free tillers, not able to speak the thing they would, liable to band into unions). Tennyson does not see that there might be an alignment that poets and workers might share.

There is another significant and, for Tennyson, dangerous factor: the tendency of trade to intrude upon the poetic margins, so that even the space Tennyson reserves for imaginative freedom is under threat. The increase of state power and wealth is envisaged, in the penultimate stanza, as spreading 'from land to land': even the remote places in which the imagination may live may be engulfed, and the 'golden sand' which might be a part of their attraction is, in this context, a metaphor for money. Utilitarian doctrine allows the poet to take himself or herself off to a margin where trade won't be disturbed by poetic visions of freedom; but the centre encroaches inexorably upon the margins.

Centre and Margins

The opposition in 'You ask me, why, though ill at ease' between near and remote places ('this region' with its 'Freedom', and 'the purple seas', 'The palms and temples of the South') signals a major strategy by which Tennyson sought to handle the divergence of political and imaginative freedoms. Finding imaginative impetus marginalized theoretically and politically in Britain, he invested it in remote places. Finding himself expected to explore states of mind, he did so by using the people and scenery of remote places, and their impact on Europeans. The convergence is recognized already in Fox's review of *Poems, Chiefly Lyrical*: in 'the analysis of particular states of mind', he says, the poet 'has provision made for an inexhaustible supply of subjects. A new world is discovered for him to conquer' (Armstrong, p. 75). In Tennyson's practice, the marginalized activity of analysing states of mind occurs repeatedly within a move to a geographical periphery where he locates kinds of experience not valued at the centre. This was not a new movement: Wordsworth had done something similar for the literary public with the image of Cumberland, and George Borrow was pursuing Gypsies and the 'wild' Welsh. At the margins of English influence might still be found, it was felt, truer imaginative vision – a way of life not yet under the sway of the dominant ideology.

The combination of place and state of mind is the whole project of 'The Lotos-Eaters'. The place is remote from the restless accumulation of the European system and its purposeful and compelled labour –

We only toil, who are the first of things,
And make perpetual moan,
Still from one sorrow to another thrown.

(lines 61–3)

(This is presented as the human condition, but plainly it does not apply to the island's inhabitants). And the state of mind which the island inspires in the mariners is similarly remote from the European system. Stanzas expounding their thoughts alternate with stanzas describing the land-scape, and the two become utterly involved with each other, especially through the music of the poem which, like the music of the island, washes across the whole experience:

There is sweet music here that softer falls
Than petals from blown roses on the grass,
Or night-dews on still waters between walls
Of shadowy granite, in a gleaming pass;
Music that gentlier on the spirit lies,
Than tired eyelids upon tired eyes.

(lines 46–51)

Sound, vision, touch and 'the spirit' are all interinvolved.

Ulysses also has the alternative of a useful life, awaken-ing people to the benefits of bourgeois freedom –

by slow prudence to make mild
A rugged people, and through soft degrees
Subdue them to the useful and the good.

But he prefers to travel to the margin which, again, is apprehended mainly as a state of mind:

I am a part of all that I have met;
Yet all experience is an arch wherethrough
Gleams that untravelled world, whose margin fades
For ever and for ever when I move.

At each move he makes, Ulysses invests what he encounters with himself, yet he must always be seeking that which is just beyond reach. That this is the characteristic strategy of metaphysics I will argue in the next chapter; also, it has specific political determinants.

This centre/margins structure is used by Tennyson repeatedly as a way of handling the tensions within current conceptions of politics and poetry. He manages an astonishing range of different emphases as he twists and turns, seeking to reorder the constraints upon him. In 'Timbuctoo', the Cambridge prize poem of 1829, he already understands that legends of paradisal places are imaginative constructs, whose validity is defined in terms of their remoteness from the ordinary operations of western society:

> And much I mused on legends quaint and old
> Which whilome won the hearts of all on Earth
> Toward their brightness, even as flame draws air;
> But had their being in the heart of Man
> As air is the life of flame.
>
> (lines 16–20)

Tennyson had been reading Hugh Murray's *Historical Account of Discoveries and Travels in Africa*, where it is suggested that the doubtful geography of the Hesperian Gardens, the Fortunate Islands and the Isles of the Blest manifests

> the operation of certain secret propensities, that are deeply lodged in the human breast. There arises involuntarily in the heart of man a longing after forms of being fairer and happier than any presented by the world before him – bright scenes which he seeks and never finds in the circuits of real existence. But imagination easily creates them in that dim boundary which separates the known from the unknown world.[40]

In 'Timbuctoo' Tennyson alludes to the uncertain geography of Atlantis and Eldorado:

> Where are ye
> Thrones of the Western wave, fair Islands green?

Where are your moonlight halls, your cedarn glooms,
The blossoming abysses of your hills?
Your flowering Capes, and your gold-sanded bays
Blown round with happy airs of odorous winds?
                                        (lines 40–5)

Where were they indeed? Because the prize poem was to be about Timbuctoo, Tennyson focused on that location, but he could see that such places represented an alternative to incorporation, offering a theme where he could sustain some of the imaginative exaltation with which Shelley had been able to invest his vision of human justice and equality.

Almost all Tennyson's remote places are threatened with or actually experience disaster. His early writing in *Poems by Two Brothers* (1827) is heavily Byronic, and hence fully alive to the possibilities of tyranny, slaughters and prophetic denunciations. Characteristically, one people is defeated, enslaved and destroyed by another – the Hindostanis by Nadir Shah, the Egyptians by the Babylonians, the Peruvians by the Spanish, the Druids by the Romans.[41] The poetic margin is always under threat: typically 'The land like an Eden before them [the invaders] is fair,/But behind them a wilderness dreary and bare' ('The Expedition of Nadir Shah into Hindostan'). 'Timbuctoo' was derived from 'Armageddon'. In 'The Lotos-Eaters', as commentators keen to reap a good moral have pointed out, there is a sense that the mariners in seeking to evade the requirements of a developed economy are infringing the prerogative of the gods, and will suffer for it. And in 'Ulysses' it is strongly hinted that this voyage – again hubristic, if we pick up allusions to Dante – is to be their last.

Of course, many of these disasters were historical: they were the result of 'civilized' intrusion upon other cultures. Tennyson had been reading Washington Irving's *Life and Voyages of Christopher Columbus* (1828), and from it he got the story for 'Anacaona' (1830). The title is the name of a queen of Haiti and 48 lines describe her island paradise in most fulsome terms. Then comes

The white man's sail, bringing
　To happy Hayti the new-comer,
Over the dark sea-marge springing,
　Floated in the silent summer.

Anacaona welcomes the voyagers and leads them 'down the
pleasant places'; but then, the poem concludes:

　No more in Xaraguay
Wandered happy Anacaona,
　The beauty of Espagnola,
　The golden flower of Hayti!

Here Tennyson disturbs by understatement: we are left to
infer the fact that the colonizers killed the queen and many
of her people. This poem should be better known; that it is
not is doubtless due to the fact that Tennyson never printed
it because he feared that the natural history might be
inaccurate – an instance of the values of the matter of fact
centre triumphing over those of the imaginative margin.

This kind of incident was by no means confined to the
Spanish, or the sixteenth century or the Americas. When
Tennyson was writing, the West Indies, as we have seen,
signified slavery and its replacement by bourgeois freedom
rather than an exotic margin. 'The Lotos-Eaters' fits better
into Tennyson's world if we envisage it situated in the last
inhabited region to be explored by Europeans, the Pacific,
which had been visited by, among others, Captain Cook in
the late eighteenth century. On Tahiti in 1769 Cook was
greeted very like Ulysses' mariners: 'No one of the Natives
made the least opposition at our landing but came to us
with all imaginable marks of friendship and submission.'[42]
The island was immediately constructed by Cook as a kind
of Eden exempt from the demands of a European economy
– 'in the article of food these people may almost be said to
be exempt from the curse of our fore fathers; scarcely can it
be said that they earn their bread with the sweat of their
brow' (I, 121). Cook's colleague Joseph Banks thought it
'an arcadia'.[43] What so attracted Europeans about Tahiti

was not lotos but the sexual availability of the islanders, which derived from both their own more relaxed attitude and the economic, military and cultural power of the intruders. Like Ulysses' mariners, European sailors tried to remain on the island: the mutiny on the Bounty originated in the sailors' resentment at leaving Tahiti after a five months' stay. In Cook's time there were probably 40,000 people on Tahiti. By 1800, because of wars and disease, especially venereal disease introduced by Europeans, not more than 16,000 were left. By the 1830s there were only 9,000 and the figure fell further to 6,000. When Gauguin arrived in the 1890s he was horrified by the hopeless inertia of the remaining islanders.[44] The destruction of purpose, personality and culture attributed by Tennyson to the lotos was achieved in actuality by European intrusion.

Tennyson's persistent dwelling on the possibility of disaster at his exotic margins may be related to his anxiety about popular disturbances and working class organization in England. Irving's account of 'a horrible massacre . . . among the populace' of Anacaona's Haiti by the Spanish leader Ovando sounds just like Peterloo: 'At the signal of Ovando, the horsemen rushed into the midst of the naked and defenceless throng, trampling them under the hoofs of their steeds, cutting them down with their swords, and transfixing them with their spears. No mercy was shown to age or sex; it was a savage and indiscriminate butchery.'[45] Tennyson might have vaguely recognized that the violence used to maintain class domination in England resembled that used abroad. But his face was set against this; he refused to believe that British liberties might be secured in the way that white American liberty was, or that British wage slaves were not so distinct from West Indian blacks; or, fundamentally, that poetry, forced into incorporation or marginalization, might make common cause with other victims of bourgeois hegemony.

The threat of destruction hanging over Tennyson's remote places is perhaps related to his sense of the vulnerability of the marginal space allowed to poetry –

because the governing centre, impelled in particular by the doctrine of free trade, was pressing continually out into the margins. This is the anxiety that surfaces in 'You ask me, why, though ill at ease':

> Though Power should make from land to land
>   The name of Britain trebly great –
>   Though every channel of the State
> Should fill and choke with golden sand –
>
> Yet waft me from the harbour-mouth . . .

The spread of 'Power . . . from land to land' encroaches even on the idea of 'golden sand'; like the poet, it sets out 'from the harbour-mouth', though he tries to make his expedition sound different through 'waft'. Tennyson cannot prevent bourgeois freedom from intruding on the margins where he locates imaginative freedom. 'Hail Briton!' opens with the same thought: the Briton is hailed 'in whatever zone' he may be, but

> Not for a power, that knows not check,
>   To spread and float an ermined pall
>   Of Empire, from the ruined wall
> Of royal Delhi to Quebec.

(lines 9–12)

This is vigorously hostile to imperial expansion. Power is unchecked and Delhi has a 'ruined wall' (deriving from the wars against the Marathas in 1803–4, when Delhi came under British administration). The 'ermined pall' may be just a rich canopy, but it suggests also the cloth spread over a hearse, and metaphorically it often means a dark cloud producing gloom. That remote place has already been invaded from the centre.

The vulnerability of exotic margins to discovery is a theme of both Washington Irving and Hugh Murray. Irving remarks that the idea of a terrestial paradise was located for a long time in the Canaries 'because discovery advanced no farther, and because these islands were so distant, and so little known, as to allow full latitude to the fictions of the poet'; and adds that 'the mystery and conjectural charm that reigned over the greatest part of the world . . . have since been completely dispelled by modern discovery.'[46] Part of Murray's argument about the geographical uncertainty of the imagined paradise is that 'we find these fairy spots successively retreating before the progress of discovery, yet finding still, in the farthest advance which ancient knowledge ever made, some remoter extremity to which they can fly.'[47] Tennyson addresses the theme in 'Timbuctoo':

> I must render up this glorious home
> To keen *Discovery*: soon yon brilliant towers
> Shall darken with the waving of her wand.
>
> (lines 239–41)

The argument is awkward, for the story of Timbuctoo requires that the city be superseded not by European adventurers but by 'Low-built, mud-walled, Barbarian settlements' (244): evidently Tennyson was determined to relate the destruction of the exotic space to discovery, to a threat from the centre to the margin.

Marginalization and incorporation presented themselves as alternative routes for poetry, then, but actually the margins were being pushed continually into more remote regions, even as industry and commerce pursued their interests across the globe, justifying themselves through the ideology of utilitarianism and political economy. Marx and Engels identified this as a fundamental process of capitalism:

> The need of a constantly expanding market for its products chases the bourgeoisie over the whole surface of the globe. It must nestle everywhere, settle everywhere, establish connections everywhere. . . . It compels all nations, on pain of extinction, to adopt the bourgeois mode of production; it compels them to introduce what it calls civilization into their midst, i.e. to become bourgeois themselves. In one word, it creates a world after its own image.[48]

Political economy actually had what Mill called an 'intel-lectual and moral' justification of this. As he put it in *Principles of Political Economy* (1848):

> Commercial adventurers from more advanced countries have generally been the first civilizers of barbarians. . . . Such communication has always been, and is peculiarly in the present age, one of the primary sources of progress. . . . And it may be said without exaggeration that the great extent and rapid increase of international trade, in being the principal guarantee of the peace of the world, is the great permanent security for the uninterrupted progress of the ideas, the institutions, and the character of the human race.[49]

The actual outcome was rather different. What hap-pened in India, Hobsbawm shows, 'was simply the virtual destruction, within a few decades, of what had been a flourishing domestic and village industry which sup-plemented the rural incomes; in other words the deindustrialization of India', making 'the peasant village itself more dependent on the single, fluctuating fortune of the harvest'.[50] Thus an economy which had been in balance with itself and with Europe was destroyed, producing a situation from which India has not yet recovered. The consequent disasters have been far greater than Tennyson could have envisaged.

The positions canvassed by the speaker in 'Locksley Hall' address just the range of issues we have considered. Disappointed in love by Amy's capitulation to 'the social wants that sin against the strength of youth' (line 59), personified by figures reminiscent of Tennyson's grand-father and uncle, he seeks a renewal of imaginative vitality in travel to distant lands. Thus his situation is the poet's: he is cut off from what might be the most significant kind of imaginative experience within society (marriage to Amy, the Shelleyan resolution) and obliged to find an alternative commitment in far-flung places. He tries to align his vision with an impetus from the 'wondrous Mother-Age' (108), hoping somehow to evade his perception that the economic and class values which produced Amy's marriage *are* those of the Age ('Every door is barred with gold, and opens but to golden keys', 100). Perhaps trade itself can be a romantic ideal: he

> Saw the heavens fill with commerce, argosies of magic sails,
> Pilots of the purple twilight, dropping down with costly bales.
>
> (lines 121–2)

Put like that, trade does not threaten the margin – rather, the margin throws its evocative mantle over trade. If Tennyson could only believe this, he would dissolve the whole dichotomy of incorporation and marginalization. The speaker even suggests, like political economists, that endless commerce will produce endless peace:

> Till the war-drum throbbed no longer, and the battle-flags were furled
> In the Parliament of man, the Federation of the world.
>
> (lines 127–8)

But the vision does not hold, and there is danger at home: 'Slowly comes a hungry people, as a lion creeping nigher' (135). He yearns instead for the solution of 'The Lotos-Eaters', an imaginative investment in peripheral spaces uncorrupted by the centre:

> Ah, for some retreat
> Deep in yonder shining Orient, where my life began to beat;
>
> Where in wild Mahratta-battle fell my father evil-starred; –
> I was left a trampled orphan, and a selfish uncle's ward.
>
> Or to burst all links of habit – there to wander far away,
> On from island unto island at the gateways of the day.
>
> (lines 153–8)

The movement here is precise. We have seen Tennyson already, in 'Hail Briton!', express reservations about British power in India, referring to 'the ruined wall/Of royal Delhi' and the wars against the Marathas in 1803–4. There was no escape in India: it was the one place the free traders were determined to incorporate directly. As Hobsbawm explains, 'with one crucial exception' the British view was:

> that a world lying open to British trade and safeguarded by the British navy from unwelcome intrusion was more cheaply exploited without the administrative costs of occupation. The crucial exception was India. . . . Its market was of growing importance and would certainly, it was held, suffer if India were left to herself. It was the key to the opening-up of the Far East, to the drug traffic [lotos?] and such other profitable activities as European businessmen wished to undertake.[51]

That is why the speaker of Tennyson's poem has to press on, to 'wander far away' in search of 'Breadths of tropic shade and palms in cluster, knots of Paradise' and 'Summer isles of Eden lying in dark-purple spheres of sea' (160, 164). He must get to where 'Never comes the trader, never floats an European flag' (161):

> There methinks would be enjoyment more than in this
>   march of mind,
> In the steamship, in the railway, in the thoughts that
>   shake mankind.

> (lines 165–6)

However, this position also proves unsustainable. The speaker cannot relinquish the idea of European superiority; he counts 'the gray barbarian lower than the Christian child' (174). He will follow the call of remote places nevertheless – 'Not in vain the distance beacons' (181) – but inspired by imagery of machinery and progress: 'Let the great world spin for ever down the ringing grooves of change' (182). In Tennyson's terms, this is no resolution.

Having failed to invest trade with the aura of the margins, the speaker will take the values of the centre to 'the distance'. The poem concludes with an image of disaster overwhelming margins and centre alike:

> Comes a vapour from the margin, blackening over
>   heath and holt,
> Cramming all the blast before it, in its breast a
>   thunderbolt.
>
> Let it fall on Locksley Hall.

(lines 191–3)

What 'Locksley Hall' helps us to see is that the ultimate threat to remote spaces comes from Tennyson himself. It is he who corrupts the exotic other by seeking to appropriate it for his poetic enterprise – which, for all that it is marginalized, is an enterprise constructed within the terms of bourgeois order. That is why, although he seeks to get beyond the politics of the European economic system, that politics keeps on reappearing, flourishing after all at the poetical margin. As Marx and Engels declare, the bourgeoisie 'creates a world after its own image', and that is precisely what Tennyson does. We might say, metaphorically, that it is a kind of colonization and trade: the poet throws his imagination out to the periphery, plants himself as securely as he can there, adapting all that he finds to his project, and brings back to the mother country a rich hoard which helps it to cope, not with the inadequacies of its economic system, but with the ideological contradictions which that system creates. Significantly, Columbus and his followers discovered qualities associated with poetry among the Haitians: their life is said to approach 'the golden state of poetical felicity', they are like 'the fabled dryads, or native nymphs and fairies of the fountains, sung by the ancient poets'.[52]

This assimilation of marginal experiences into centrist language typifies relations between Europe and what we would now call the third world. Even as the discoverers arrived in Tahiti, they translated what they found into their own terms. The first thought of Joseph Banks in Tahiti was: 'in short, the scene we saw was the truest picture of an arcadia of which we were going to be kings that the imagination can form.'[53] At first sight this seems contradictory: is not the idea of an arcadia destroyed as soon as one imagines being king over it? But the contradiction occurs earlier than that, in the attempt to fix another society through the European poetic idea of arcadia. Louis de Bougainville in the account of his visit in 1768 anticipates even more closely Tennyson's way of adapting remote places and people to Greek mythology:

> The girl carelessly dropt a cloth, which covered her, and appeared to the eyes of all beholders, such as Venus shewed herself to the Phrygian shepherd, having, indeed, the celestial form of that goddess. . . . At last our cares succeeded in keeping these bewitched fellows [mariners] in order, though it was no less difficult to keep the command of ourselves.[54]

Edward Said has explained how the *whole idea* of 'the Orient' was constructed to serve the ideological convenience of Europe. 'The Orient was overvalued for its pantheism, its spirituality, its stability, its longevity, its primitivity, and so forth' – this is the main effect working through Tennyson's writing. But there are traces also of 'a counterresponse' by which 'the Orient suddenly appeared lamentably under-humanized, antidemocratic, backward, barbaric, and so forth'.[55] Tennyson manifests this also: in the violence which overtakes his remote peoples, in the sense of something flawed in their lifestyles, in the shame of the 'Locksley Hall' speaker at the idea that he might 'herd with narrow foreheads, vacant of our glorious gains' (line 175). 'Orientalism', Said argues, 'depends for its strategy on this flexible *positional* superiority, which puts the Westerner in a whole series of possible relationships with the Orient without ever losing him the upper hand' (p. 7). Tennyson's use of remote places was in the service of a wider project, calculated to help Europe handle its own ideological problems, and especially those associated with its domination of the rest of the world.

This can be seen only too well in Tennyson's view of why Ireland should be subjected to England:

> The Teuton has no poetry in his nature like the Celt, and this makes the Celt much more dangerous in politics, for he yields more to his imagination than his common sense. . . . [Ireland] has absolute freedom now, and a more than full share in the government of one of the mightiest empires in the world. Whatever she may say, she is not only feudal, but oriental, and loves those in authority over her to have the iron hand in the silken glove. (*Memoir*, p. 701).

The whole narrative is here. Ireland is on the margins of England, and so can be invested with the poetry and imagination which are to be held in check at the centre; but because this marginal space is so close to England it cannot be allowed national freedom – only bourgeois freedom, which Tennyson declares it has. Despite this freedom, however, Ireland is to be dealt with by an iron hand, and this is justified by appealing to another supposed attribute of the 'oriental', its love of feudal control. Furthermore, once Ireland has been thus incorporated, it can be read back as an undesirable aspect of the centre, contributing, with the lower classes, to the mysterious forces which threaten bourgeois freedom from within – 'that unstable Celtic blood' in 'Hail Briton!', 'The blind hysterics of the Celt' in *In Memoriam* (109).

The idea that the poet is not, finally, the opposite of the discoverer-killer-trader-enslaver-colonist, but is continuous with him, was already set up for Tennyson by Irving, who presents Columbus as a kind of poet. 'In Columbus', Irving writes, 'were singularly combined the practical and the poetical;' 'his poetical temperament is discernible throughout all his writings and in all his actions. It spread a golden and glorious world around him, and tinged everything with its own gorgeous colours'.[56] Hence Irving insists that 'lofty anticipations . . . elevated Columbus above all mercenary interests – at least for a while' (II, 504). Nevertheless, he and his followers cruelly oppressed the Indians. The poetic intrusion initiates the sequence which leads to trading, enslavement, colonization and the massacre of Anacaona's people. The poetic spirit is the advance guard of capitalism and imperialism, and cannot escape this involvement.

The final effect is a domination which is cultural and linguistic as well as commercial. Francis Palgrave's preface to *The Golden Treasury* (published in 1861 with Tennyson's advice) concluded with the thought: 'wherever the Poets of England are honoured, wherever the dominant language of the world is spoken, it is hoped that they will find fit audience'.[57] So Ulysses, like Tennyson and Columbus, takes with him the dominant language of the world and imposes its cultural requirements wherever he goes. He invests all that he meets with himself, in an imperialism of the imagination:

> I am a part of all that I have met;
> Yet all experience is an arch wherethrough
> Gleams that untravelled world, whose margin fades
> For ever and for ever when I move.

Ulysses *is* the hegemonic: he is the colonizer who requires ever more remote margins to sustain his enterprise. The opposition with Telemachus and 'the useful and the good' holds only to a point. Hence the melancholy of the setting forth, the sense that they must eventually reach eternity, the total involvement of the project with death. Ulysses is the source of destruction: everytime he arrives he brings the centre with him, and the margin has thus to move on, fading 'For ever and for ever when I move'. So it is with the poet's push towards remote places, which embraces a margin defined as such by the centre. Even so, although it cannot transcend the hegemonic it may, wittingly and unwittingly, help to expose the oppressiveness of its operations.

The Marginalization of Tennyson

To many readers this chapter will seem surprising – it will
seem that Hallam was on the right lines when he accepted
lack of political influence as a fair price for the untrammel-
led maintenance of the poet's exclusive vision, and that
Tennyson showed great imaginative intuition when he
sought out distant scenes which might afford some alternative perspective on industrial society. The modern reader is
likely to appreciate Hallam's position because it is not far
from the dominant attitude in literary criticism. In fact, it
contributes specifically to the tendency, indicated in the
previous chapter, to separate Literature from its historical
context and from political and social concerns. The rapidly
developing bourgeois hegemony could not tolerate the
Shelleyan conjunction and offered the choice of relegation,
incorporation and marginalization. Hallam chose the
latter: he was proud that Tennyson came 'before the public
unconnected with any political party' (Armstrong, pp. 92–
3), and sought to establish a distinct and privileged domain
for poetry. The outcome is the notion that poetry is
characterized by its capacity to say little about the
everyday relations between people and, even less, about the
power system whose pressures and limits ultimately determine them. But this move does not escape utilitarianism;
on the contrary, it is structured by it; nor has mainstream
literary criticism of the twentieth century passed beyond
that structure.

What has been happening since the late nineteenth
century, and was rendered decisive by Modernism, is a
realignment of the possibilities such that straightforward
incorporation is no longer acceptable within the main
discourses which control the institutions of poetry. The
marginalized idea – Hallam's exclusive figure of refined
sensibility – has come to seem the paradigm of the poet,
within an increasing specialization of Literature as the
province of 'the arts', an international metropolitan avant

garde, and academic study. The incorporative idea –
commanding the sympathies of unnumbered hearts – has
been assigned (with certain exceptions which stand out as
exceptions) to the middlebrow.[58]

The line from Hallam's essay through Yeats to Modernism has long been discussed, for instance by Marshall
McLuhan and Frank Kermode.[59] They have demonstrated
a continuity of theory and practice which enshrines and
repeats the utilitarian framework. Gérard Genette in a
parallel perception has remarked the opposition between
'utilitarian' and 'poetic' language in Valéry, and followed it
through Claudel, Proust, Sartre and Jakobson.[60] The same
basic thought underlies T. S. Eliot's comment: 'When a
poet's mind is perfectly equipped for its work, it is
constantly amalgamating disparate experience; the ordinary man's experience is chaotic, irregular, fragmentary.'[61]
And I. A. Richards claims that 'the arts' record:

> subtle or recondite experience [which] are for most
> men incommunicable and indescribable, though
> social conventions or terror of the loneliness of the
> human situation may make us pretend the contrary.
> In the arts we find the record in the only form in which
> these things can be recorded of the experiences which
> have seemed worth having to the most sensitive and
> discriminating persons.[62]

This assumption underlies the relationship between poetry
and essentialist humanism, as I described it in chapter 1.
'Poetry' is offered as a repudiation of utilitarianism, as that
which opposes its values, but in fact it is its correlative.
Each uses the other to establish its own status and
functions, but this enables utilitarianism to claim by far the
more comprehensive application.

If we would challenge the marginality of Tennyson,
Literature and the critical discourses in which they are
implicated, making them accessible to wider cultural
modes and responsive to the serious questions which face
humankind, then we must attempt not to reproduce the

ruling constructs but to get round behind them. This will mean, as I have been trying to do, attending to some different poems, looking at familiar poems in different ways, applying more powerful theories, and relating the poetry to other contemporary practices. The next chapter pursues the same project, by investigating the metaphysical strategies through which Tennyson characteristically tried to attain secure notions of self and ultimate reality.

3 'The Mortal Limits of the Self'

Naming the Nameless

Central to Victorian poetry was the relationship between the individual consciousness and a supposed ultimate reality. Here the poet might claim a distinctive authority that did not impinge on the business of cotton spinning. If everyday relations and power structures are not his or her province, transcendental experience surely must be. In this domain poetic privilege is surely justified, for here is the purest state of mind, the final frontier of human experience. This theme, and the precise form it took, were fully acceptable to many of Tennyson's contemporaries. Writers since the time of the Reformation had often reflected independently on questions of religion, and Blake, Wordsworth and Shelley, at the peak of their powers, had been profoundly radical. In Tennyson's time religious debate became general, with the spread of education, the growth of scientific knowledge and publishing, and the inability of the Anglican Church to cope with the rate of social and demographic change. Engagement with matters of 'faith and doubt' seemed a responsible move for a poet. It was also temperamentally attractive to Tennyson, perhaps the more so because of the disorientating political conditions described in the previous chapter.

In a letter of 1874, responding to a query about 'revelations through anaesthetics', Tennyson wrote:

> A kind of waking trance I have frequently had, quite up from boyhood, when I have been all alone. This has generally come upon me thro' repeating my own name two or three times to myself silently, till all at once, as it were out of the intensity of the consciousness of individuality, the individuality itself seems to dissolve and fade away into boundless being, and this not a confused state, but the clearest of the clearest, and surest of the surest, the weirdest of the weirdest, utterly beyond words, where death was an almost laughable impossibility, the loss of personality (if so it were) seeming no extinction but the only true life. (*Memoir*, p. 268)

Increasingly, Tennyson was haunted by the thought that this kind of experience might underwrite something like God and the soul, as they had traditionally been authorized by the churches and the Bible. In 'The Ancient Sage' (1885), the sage reads from a scroll which he has taken from a young follower and argues against its scepticism. He offers as climactic evidence for the existence of an ultimate reality an experience like Tennyson's:

> And more, my son! for more than once when I
> Sat all alone, revolving in myself
> The word that is the symbol of myself,
> The mortal limit of the Self was loosed,
> And past into the Nameless, as a cloud
> Melts into Heaven. I touched my limbs, the limbs
> Were strange not mine – and yet no shade of doubt,
> But utter clearness, and through such loss of Self
> The gain of such large life as matched with ours
> Were Sun to spark – unshadowable in words,
> Themselves but shadows of a shadow-world.[1]

The preoccupation here with individual identity, and the yearning for an ultimate ground of fullness of being, are related – both as two poles of the one opposition, and as twin attempts to push past language to a reality beyond it.

Tennyson's personal anxieties about identity and meaning, fuelled by historical conditions, pick up on a traditional theme. The passage re-enacts the fundamental project of western metaphysics: the attempt to locate a final, secure ground of meaning – in the self, a transcendent other, or, best of all, in a relationship between the two.

Tennyson's account echoes that of Plotinus, the third century Neo-Platonic philosopher: 'Many times it has happened: lifted out of the body into myself; becoming external to all other things and self-encentred; beholding a marvellous beauty; then, more than ever, assured of community with the loftiest order; enacting the noblest life, acquiring identity with the divine.'[2] Tennyson was inclined to take such similarities as evidence of the significance of his trances (*Memoir*, p. 168). Alternatively, we might view the similarities as evidence that Tennyson has construed his physical experience within the framework of ideas made available by his culture – that the significance that can be ascribed to experience is determined culturally. And from this we might infer, rightly I think, that Tennyson's idea that his trances might point towards a meaning beyond culture is, precisely and inevitably, a chimera.

A major impetus behind recent critical theories has been the thought that experience is constructed culturally, in language. Saussurean structuralism points out that language is always differential – founded in oppositions which say finally that *a* is *a* because it is not *b*. Thus language actually constructs the distinctions which it appears to identify in the world. This theory does not address the question of whether the world is there or not, but, rather, what kinds of things we can say and think about it. Our perceptions, let alone statements, are mediated through the grid of language into which we are born and which arranges sense impressions, abstract concepts and human relationships into schemes of significance.[3]

Jacques Lacan has argued that the self, also, has no essential existence, that it is formed as the infant moves into language, that it identifies itself only in terms of the symbolic system of the society into which it is received.[4]

And Marxists observe, in notions that the world and the self are *essentially* thus or thus, ideological strategies working to persuade men and women that the present order of things is necessarily so.

In the light of this body of theory, Tennyson's concern with his own name, and with the possible existence of 'the Nameless', appears as an anxiety about the constructedness of reality in language, and as an attempt to move beyond it. It is in this sense that his approach is metaphysical. As Jacques Derrida has argued, metaphysics strives always to bridge or efface the gap between language and reality and to control the play of language, in the hope, always just beyond fulfilment, that language can achieve 'full presence, the reassuring foundation, the origin and end of play'.[5] Tennyson's writings are fascinating in relation to the whole issue of the construction of reality in language, for they often encourage specific awareness of its implications, though usually drawing back from the fullest conclusions. His language exhibits the pressures of handling the most problematic and provocative aspects of the metaphysical project (chapter 4 will be about how Tennyson attempts to fill up language, rendering it more dense and real). The earnestness of Tennyson's engagement and the precariousness of his resolutions perhaps manifest a certain desperation. Also, they challenge and inform the reader.

Tennyson's poetry is saturated with attempts to name the Nameless. In 'The Two Voices' it is given as a characteristic of 'man' that 'His heart forebodes a mystery:/ He names the name Eternity' (lines 290–1). Tennyson alludes to one of his trances at the turning point of *In Memoriam*, in section 95: 'And all at once it seemed at last/The living soul was flashed on mine'; in section 124 the poet recalls:

> And what I am beheld again
>   What is, and no man understands,

And out of darkness came the hands
That reach through nature, moulding men.

'What is' cannot be given a name, but finally it seems to promise 'In the deep night, that all is well' (section 126).

Tennyson knows that the notion of ultimate being is fundamentally bound up with the inability of language to formulate that notion. In 'The Ancient Sage' words are 'Themselves but shadows of a shadow-world'; in *In Memoriam* they 'half reveal/And half conceal the Soul within' (section 5). The assumption is that there is a reality beyond language which may be glimpsed but not expressed; in fact, what actually happens in these instances is that ultimate being is gestured towards precisely *through* the complaint about the inadequacy of language. So in *In Memoriam* (95) the reality of the poet's vision is set off against the dulling effect of language. His 'trance' is 'cancelled, stricken through with doubt' (notice the language of writing), and he declares:

Vague words! but ah, how hard to frame
In matter-moulded forms of speech,
Or even for intellect to reach
Through memory that which I became.

Tennyson is ready to recognize that language is a human construction because he can use this to point beyond it, to a realm which is not to be comprised in language. In 'The Higher Pantheism' he speaks of the physical world as a language *because* it manifests our separation from 'Him who reigns':

Earth, these solid stars, this weight of body and limb,
Are not they sign and symbol of thy division from him?

Language is of the physical world and it manifests our exile from ultimate reality.

Hence the juxtaposition of the mortal name and 'the Nameless' in 'The Ancient Sage':

> > revolving in myself
> The word that is the symbol of myself,
> The mortal limit of the Self was loosed,
> And past into the Nameless.

The sage separates his self from the symbol of his self: he does it by revolving that symbol in himself so that the outer (the name) becomes the inner. But what is then reached is not the self deeper inside, but the Nameless, that which is beyond 'The mortal limit' and the language which demarcates that limit. So the inner is transformed into a new outer. The non-mortal quality of this state is indicated by its lack of a name, for to be in language is to be in the mortal condition. Of course, the sage can only gesture towards this state beyond language, for 'the Nameless' *is a name*. But this is in the nature of the metaphysical project: the ultimate ground is always that which is just beyond reach, and language can only point beyond itself. Browning put this very clearly when Andrea del Sarto exclaims: 'Ah, but a man's reach should exceed his grasp,/Or what's a Heaven for?'[6]

As the sage reaches towards the Nameless, in the passage quoted, language progressively reveals its inadequacy so that a further state, just eluding containment, can be intimated. Initially language names the individual, and its intensive use ('revolving in myself/The word') looses the limits of 'the Self' and affords access to 'the Nameless'. But then the ultimate reality is defined in terms of its inaccessibility to language, and by the end of the passage the adequacy of language even to the human world is in question: words are 'Themselves but shadows of a shadow-world'. Yet the distinction is not allowed to be watertight; it cannot be, for after all there is no final escape from language, and the sage returns to the world:

> . . . And past into the Nameless, as a cloud
> Melts into Heaven. I touched my limbs, the limbs
> Were strange not mine – and yet no shade of doubt,

> But utter clearness, and through such loss of Self
> The gain of such large life as matched with ours
> Were Sun to spark – unshadowable in words,
> Themselves but shadows of a shadow-world.

Concepts and images interlock so that the second term picks up the first and augments it, at the same time seeming to abandon it: the 'cloud/Melts into Heaven', with the capital H turning the physical analogy into a premonition of its own spiritual implications; 'my limbs' become 'the limbs . . . not mine'. The replacements become more definite – though still negatively propounded – as the syntax continues to extend itself, as far as a possible stopping point at 'Sun to spark'; then the play on shadows runs the same effect backwards, depositing the sage back in the 'shadow-world' of the follower and his scroll – 'I touch thy world again' (line 249). The language strives to name the Nameless by undermining progressively its own claim to reference, requiring, as the condition for a return to the 'mortal limit', a recognition that language itself constructs that limit at third remove from ultimate being.

There are two ways of regarding this linguistic strategy. If one is inclined to credit the ultimate reality it seeks to address, one will think that the poet has pointed to it as fully as is possible. If one is disinclined to credit it, one will see it as a suppressed admission of failure behind which may lurk all manner of further doubts and anxieties. The latter was Swinburne's response, who wrote beneath 'The Higher Pantheism': 'God, whom we see not, is; and God, who is not, we see:/Fiddle we know, is diddle: and diddle is possibly dee.'[7] These interpretive alternatives are always available: one may accept Tennyson's position or warily read through it, disclosing its strategy.

In 'The Ancient Sage' Tennyson moves boldly to address the major flaw in the kind of binary opposition which the sage, in the manner of the metaphysical tradition, has been constructing. The flaw is that the terms can all too easily be reversed; and so the sceptical scroll reverses the sage's light/dark imagery: 'Night and Shadow rule below/When only Day should reign.' The sage replies by admitting the problem:

> Some say, the Light was father of the Night,
> And some, the Night was father of the Light.
> No night no day! – I touch thy world again –
> No ill no good! such counter-terms, my son,
> Are border races, holding each its own
> By endless war.

(lines 247–52)

The two terms have to fight, which is how each establishes its identity. This insight approaches Derrida's analysis of how such oppositions are secretly parasitic upon each other. Metaphysics imagines that by examining and revealing the terms of such an opposition, it is making progress; but in reality it is merely confirming the initial delimitation of the field, and the exclusion of other factors.[8]

It is bold of Tennyson to confront this issue, for his own thought works continuously through such binaries: language/self, self/ultimate being, inner/outer, shadow/sun, doubt/belief. But the confrontation is not sustained. Tennyson sidesteps it:'The Ancient Sage' continues:

> but night enough is there
> In yon dark city: get thee back . . .
> . . . and help thy fellow men.

The light/dark opposition is shifted back into purely mortal terms – what people make of their cities – and its pretensions to point towards ultimate being are set aside for the goal of work in the world. This is perhaps a move we would welcome, but the idea of the Nameless is left as, implicitly, a higher level of experience which somehow ratifies such good work in the city.

Tennyson's willingness to expose his sage to questioning is not uncourageous. If the modern reader has difficulty seeing that, it is because the terms of the debate no longer seem very important, but the reader who ridicules the Victorians' faith and doubt may be far less ready to question his or her own ruling concepts. Although Tennyson seems, in my judgement, to want the sage to win the argument, by permitting questions he allows the reader scope to move, and opens up the possibility that the reader will find what was supposed to be the weaker argument to be the stronger. So T. S. Eliot declared of *In Memoriam*, 'Its faith is a poor thing, but its doubt is a very intense experience' (*Selected Prose*, p. 172). For all this, faith/doubt constructs a metaphysical opposition, whichever way we tilt it. The point is not how or whether we decide between the two, but the centring of this opposition, so powerfully that other questions seem to be squeezed out. This is apparent when Tennyson himself reverses the terms: 'There lives more faith in honest doubt,/Believe me, than in half the creeds' (*In Memoriam*, 96). 'Believe me', redolent with earnestness and authenticity, exposes what is happening here: commitment to doubt is being offered as a new, superior brand of faith (so Eliot said this may 'justly be called a religious poem'). Faith and doubt are mutually supporting constructs: they sustain between them the notion that people need an authority beyond the human to make sense of their lives, and thus efface other ways of thinking about the world.

Learning the Use of 'I'

The individual self is supposed to provide the starting-point for the vision of the Nameless; it is offered as the first term against which the second is defined. Modern theory, above all, denies the autonomy of the subjective self.

The idea of individual subjectivity, as a given which is undetermined and unconstructed and hence a ground of meaning and coherence, is one of the main tenets of conventional nineteenth and twentieth century thought. In Literature, from the Romantics onwards, poetry authenticates itself in terms of the poet's consciousness; and the realist novel, as a framework of understanding at least, assumes that its characters are the sources of actions and the place where actions have their principal effects. As a critical notion, the autonomous self is elaborated conveniently by William Walsh, who enumerates as the meanings of 'character': 'the source of action and, in particular, of habitual action'; 'individuality, the incommunicable self'; and 'the person directed towards moral ends'.[9] Of course, as soon as this way of thinking is established its problems are opened up – not least in the novels and poems which partly depend upon it; nevertheless, the autonomous human subject is the starting-point. It is also the critical construct in the faith/doubt opposition: as ecclesiastical and rationalist authority weakened, belief became something to be tested and affirmed in the authentic self.

It is not enough to analyse the autonomous self merely as a philosophical mistake: its significance is political. The constitution of the idea of the individual in the eighteenth century was a progressive stage in the sequence by which the bourgeoisie, spearheaded often by radical intellectuals, repudiated a corrupt aristocratic rule in the name of the rights of each person – or, at least, of each European male – to pursue legitimate goals without the interference of arbitrary authority, and to contribute to the good republic on the basis of individual rational decisions. Nevertheless, the idea of the individual made it all too easy to slide away from political objectives when, as for instance in the French Revolution, they proved problematic, and to narrow the range of sympathies to those of like mind (i.e. the same class). The individual, eventually, was perceived as the opposite of the social and the political, as a site of essential human values to which those 'public' discourses could contribute little and from which they might well detract. In this sequence Tennyson's position is transitional. He addresses political issues in his poetry, though often by referring them to the individual (in *In Memoriam*, for instance, confidence in the future of the political order depends on the poet's sense of a continuing relationship with Hallam). And the poems which Tennyson probably regarded as his most profound construct the individual/ universal dichotomy which, I have argued, effaces the political and the historical.

In relation to the discussion so far, the issue of the self is the same as that of ultimate reality: whether there is any such entity, whether the name attached to it has any secure referent. Jacques Lacan has argued in psychoanalytic terms that the self is not innate but acquired: 'When the human baby learns to say "me" and "I" it is only acquiring these designations from someone and somewhere else, from the world which perceives and names it.'[10] The infant's own name is part of the differential system of language which I have already described, and the identity signalled by that name is equally acquired as the child moves into language. The child does not discover and develop a pre-existing identity, it receives an identity constructed in the world. Initially the infant experiences a sense of wholeness and harmony which it derives from the security of the relationship with the mother. The entrance into language and identity is founded in the loss of this imaginary wholeness: the belief that there must be a point of harmony and certainty persists, but attempts to locate it inevitably incorporate the split which they would heal.

By repeating his own name – 'revolving in myself/The word that is the symbol of myself' – Tennyson's sage loosens the king-pin of the sense of identity, in a quest for the ideal imaginary wholeness which, Freud and Lacan claim, precedes identity. This might lead to the discovery that the self is a construction which is always in language and so always threatened by language, that it cannot be any essential entity and therefore cannot form the basis for locating ultimate being. But Tennyson veers away from such a conclusion by projecting the wholeness of the imaginary self onto a supposed ultimate reality.

In earlier poems, the instability of the self and the construction of identity as the infant moves into language are matters for confusion and despondency. The Lady of Shalott does not live in the world, but weaves her web from the reflection in a mirror. Her name and 'Camelot' are the twin refrain words, but she cannot relate the two – cannot locate a coherent sense of her self in the world. When she finally decides she is 'half sick of shadows', she writes 'The Lady of Shalott' around the prow of a boat and floats down to Camelot: she claims her name as a necessary prelude to entrance into social life, but the project is doomed. The concluding stanza as Tennyson originally published the poem makes clear the lady's claim to enter language and social identity:

> There lay a parchment on her breast,
> That puzzled more than all the rest,
>   The wellfed wits at Camelot.
> 'The web was woven curiously
> The charm is broken utterly,
> Draw near and fear not – this is I,
>   The Lady of Shalott'.

The Lady acknowledges to the society of Camelot that the coherent web she was weaving in her self-referential isolation has to break, and the illusion with it: thus she can claim 'this is I'. But her claim is disallowed – both in that her communication achieves only puzzlement, and in that she is dead, no longer a 'self' at all.

'Supposed Confessions of a Second-Rate Sensitive Mind' is ostensibly about the loss of religious faith but, as D. J. Palmer has pointed out, it is mainly about 'individuation, when the mind grows to self-awareness and loses its undifferentiated sense of being one with the world-beyond-self'.[11] The speaker's present crisis of identity – 'I am void,/Dark, formless, utterly destroyed' (lines 121–2) – is contrasted with 'the infant's dawning year' (line 67):

Thrice happy state again to be
The trustful infant on the knee!
Who lets his rosy fingers play
About his mother's neck, and knows
Nothing beyond his mother's eyes.

(lines 40–4)

This passage is unclear about the kind of identity it attributes to the infant: he is happy and trustful, but totally dependent on 'his mother's eyes'. This may amount to a Lacanian sense of the constructedness of self. As Jacqueline Rose puts it: 'The mother does not (as in D. W. Winnicott's account) mirror the child to itself; she grants an image *to* the child'.[12] That identity may be to this degree dependent on the mother is again in play when the speaker says he beheld

Thy mild eyes upraised, that knew
The beauty and repose of faith,
And the clear spirit shining through.

(lines 74–6)

The thought that there is no identity other than that which is imparted may contribute to the speaker's distress and bafflement at the withdrawal of the mother: 'Oh! wherefore do we grow awry/From roots which strike so deep? . . . Myself? Is it thus? Myself?' (lines 77–8, 86). The poem ends in frustration and despondency:

O weary life! O weary death!
O spirit and heart made desolate!
O damned vacillating state!

Tennyson's preoccupation with identity would seem to indicate a particular degree of psychological desperation. In 1923, Harold Nicolson overturned the image of the conventional Victorian laureate with his intuition of Tennyson's psychological state:

One would prefer not to fall back upon the jargon of the psycho-analysts, but the application of the

Freudian system to the case of Tennyson is quite
illuminating. For Tennyson was afraid of a great
many things: predominantly he was afraid of death,
and sex, and God. And in all these matters he
endeavoured instinctively to sublimate his terrors by
enunciating the beliefs which he desired to feel, by
dwelling upon the solutions by which he would like
to be convinced.[13]

Since then, successive biographies have displayed Tennyson as a strange, unstable individual, immobilized by
depression and haunted by fear of epilepsy, taking hydro-
pathic 'cures' which involved 'rolling the naked patient in a
wet sheet laid on two blankets, which were then folded
around him until he was powerless to move'. Martin,
Tennyson's recent biographer, links the trances with
mental illness rather than ultimate being.[14]

In *The Princess* Tennyson himself gives a medical context
for the trances: the prince is subject to 'weird seizures':

On a sudden in the midst of men and day,
And while I walked and talked as heretofore,
I seemed to move among a world of ghosts,
And feel myself the shadow of a dream.
Our great court-Galen poised his gilt-head cane,
And pawed his head, and muttered 'catalepsy'.

(I, 15–20)

'And feel myself the shadow of a dream' is the language of
the sage's vision, but here it denotes a disability. The 'weird
seizures' occur at each main juncture in the action, and in
the climactic battle the prince falls into 'some mystic
middle state' (VI, 2) such that his survival is doubtful. This
condition is recognized as like that of the infant:

but I,
Deeper than those weird doubts could reach me, lay
Quite sundered from the moving Universe,
Nor knew what eye was on me, nor the hand
That nursed me, more than infants in their sleep.

(VII, 35–9)

'The moving Universe' could be the ultimate reality of *In Memoriam* (95) and 'The Ancient Sage', but here there is no route through to it from the dissolved self. The resolution, instead, is the conventional one of the love of a good woman in the world. The princess, although she suspects that the prince is really seeking the security of the infant's relationship with the mother ('It seems you love to cheat yourself with words:/This mother is your model', VII, 314–5), agrees to marry him, and the trances are dispelled.

All the passages referring to the prince's seizures were added to *The Princess* in 1851, immediately after the publication of *In Memoriam* and Tennyson's marriage. These events seem to have released him to write of the trances as 'catalepsy' and to acknowledge a psycho-sexual dimension to them. If the prince's trajectory indicates Tennyson's belief that his trances, and the anxieties about identity which they provoked might cease, it seems he was mistaken. The Nameless was the alternative solution, and Tennyson had begun to develop it in *In Memoriam*.

The process by which Tennyson came to relate the infant's entrance into language and identity with the idea of ultimate being, and the problem in which this involved him, are apparent in section 45:

> The baby new to earth and sky,
>   What time his tender palm is prest
>   Against the circle of the breast,
> Has never thought that 'this is I':
>
> But as he grows he gathers much,
>   And learns the use of 'I' and 'me',
>   And finds 'I am not what I see,
> And other than the things I touch'.
>
> So rounds he to a separate mind
>   From whence clear memory may begin,
>   As through the frame that binds him in
> His isolation grows defined.

> This use may lie in blood and breath,
>   Which else were fruitless of their due,
>   Had man to learn himself anew
> Beyond the second birth of Death.[15]

The movement of this poem is subtle and significant. The ideal imaginary harmony of the breast precedes the move into language and identity, but this move initially seems quite positive – it is gathering, learning, finding. The third stanza enacts a change of direction. The language of growth continues in the first two lines – 'So rounds he', 'clear memory' — but the last two lines shift to ideas of confinement and alienation: 'As through the frame that binds him in/His isolation grows defined'. To be *defined* – determined in form and limits, given a precise and fixed meaning – is to be isolated.

The last stanza leaps suddenly to the thought that the only purpose of earthly individuation is that it sets us up for life after death. What the poet has in mind, in the context of the surrounding sections, is the loss of Hallam and the possibility of renewed intimacy with him. To be a mortal individual is to experience isolation and loss, but identity may have a purpose in an after-life; the 'second birth of Death' will not need to initiate again the entry into language.

This idea might seem to solve all Tennyson's problems at a stroke, but it is not sufficiently comprehensive (let alone credible). Such a projection of mortal identity onto eternity does not afford a conception of ultimate being powerful enough to deal with the full scope of the poet's distress. By remaining within the definition of human life in language, it actually impedes the ascent into the realm of the Nameless. So, two sections later, Tennyson raises the notion that life after death will consist of a merging into a 'general Soul':

> That each, who seems a separate whole,
>   Should move his rounds, and fusing all
>   The skirts of self again, should fall
> Remerging in the general Soul,

Is faith as vague as all unsweet:
   Eternal form shall still divide
   The eternal soul from all beside;
And I shall know him when we meet.

(section 47)

Division is preferable to ultimate being if it offers personal reunion with Hallam. But ultimate being still has an ineluctable claim: so Tennyson compromises and envisages

Upon the last and sharpest height,
   Before the spirits fade away,
   Some landing-place, to clasp and say,
'Farewell! We lose ourselves in light'.

This sequence in *In Memoriam* reveals the fundamentally unsatisfactory implications of the self/Nameless opposition. Immediately Tennyson has described how he induces a trance by repeating his name, he realizes that to relinquish individuality for a sense of ultimate being may be a bad bargain. As he told his son: 'But in a moment, when I come back to my normal state of "sanity", I am ready to fight for *mein liebes Ich* [my beloved self], and hold that it will last for æons of æons' (*Memoir*, p. 268). The trap in which Tennyson is caught is this: that the more he resorts to ultimate being to validate this mortal life and its meanings, the further he is forced away from life and the human relationships which might help to secure his sense of identity. The Nameless affords an answer only at the expense of abolishing the question. Tennyson's problem is not his inability to believe, but that there is no coherent belief that will cope with all his needs. He has intuited that identity is constructed in language, and that language inevitably holds us at one remove from the reality which is supposed to lie beyond it. But he casts around continually for a position somehow beyond language. It is not to be found.

Deconstruction and Materialism

The arguments and techniques of analysis in this chapter derive, broadly, from the work of Jacques Derrida and Jacques Lacan. This kind of criticism, which is beginning to seek out Tennyson's poetry, attracted by his hesitation between Romanticism and symbolism (see the next chapter), is often in danger of slipping into a nostalgia for the metaphysics it claims to displace. Thus it reasserts metaphysical priorities even while lamenting the impossibility of satisfying them.

Geoffrey Hartman in *Saving the Test* uses 'The Lady of Shalott' to ponder 'the wish to put ourselves in an unmediated relation to whatever "really" is, to know something absolutely'. This, he says, 'means a desire to be defined totally: marked or named once and for all, fixed in or by a word, and so – paradoxically – made indifferent'.[16] That last phrase is revealing: in it lurks a hint of tragic loss. Hartman knows that the quest for metaphysical grounding must be delusory, but he retrieves it by valorizing the suffering psyche. This sense is reinforced and developed in language like this: '"I am half sick of shadows", says the Lady of Shalott, and turns from her mirror to the reality of advent. She did not know that by her avertedness, by staying within representation, she had postponed death' (p. 110). Such writing comes trailing clouds of religiosity, it is redolent of the exposed soul's perilous quest for transcendent reality. Hartman produces a renewed investment in the individual consciousness, centring on its quasi-spiritual disappointment that the finality of the logos is to be achieved only in death. This approach is structured, disablingly, in terms of the metaphysics of the essential self which it claims to deconstruct.

Hartman also restores a version of the nameless ultimate reality – it is to be intuited in the artwork itself. As with subjectivity, Hartman manages to find ground for celebration in the very impossibility of fixing language: 'The most art can do, as a mirror of language, is to burn through, in its cold way, the desire for self-definition, fullness of grace, presence; simply to expose the desire to own one's own name, to inhabit it numinously in the form of "proper" noun, words, or the signatory act each poem aspires to be' (*Saving the Text*, p. 110). So the poem triumphs over absence by making us experience it. Yet Hartman wants to go further still. He observes:

> Poem and lady remain immaculate though web, mirror, or spell may break. Such impassibility is perhaps part of the infection, an unresolved narcissism of festering lily or psyche. Yet this liaison between specular and poetic is precisely what fosters the illusion of completeness and so the attractive fetish we call a poem. For a moment the et cetera of language is absorbed into that fetish: remnant and rhyme coincide. (p. 111)

The poem offers, briefly, tantalisingly, impossibly, the glimpse of a point at which language and meaning coincide.

Of course, Hartman's language is hesitant, provisional, even self-cancelling. Nonetheless, it re-enacts three movements which we have already identified. First, such precarious pointing towards the moment of coincidence is just what we saw Tennyson doing with the Nameless: we know that the ultimate ground is real *because* it just eludes the secure grasp of mortal language. Second, the trembling uncertainty about whether the poem does or does not transcend 'the et cetera of language' produces an opposition on the model of faith/doubt. It doesn't really matter on which side we come down: either way the metaphysical framework is established, occupying the ground which might otherwise be taken by a materialist analysis. Third, Hartman's approach remains trapped in the utilitarian assumptions discussed in the previous chapter. In the manner of Arthur Hallam and the subsequent tradition, he envisages poetry as the fragile transcendence of the ordinary conditions of language, the insight of a visionary sensibility working at the margins of human experience, quarantined from the main concerns of economic and political life.

The present study aspires to materialist deconstruction. Notions of secure subjective identity and transcendent reality are deconstructed, not so that they can reemerge, newly strengthened, in literary criticism, but so that we may be wary of such mystifications. And the construction of reality and the human subject is analysed so that writing can be referred to the discourses – rooted in history, ideology and power – through which it receives and transmits meaning.

4   Strategies of Language and Subjectivity

Filling Up the Sign

When I was working on the language of Tennyson's poetry in the late 1960s I took as my leading theoretical position this:

> Poetry is more densely structured than ordinary language; simply to follow the sequence of the argument is not to exhaust the meaning of the lines. The elements of poetic language are so presented as to invite us to perceive further relationships between them such that the whole poem becomes a complex web of inter-connecting meanings working almost simultaneously.[1]

I now see that this position effaces the extent to which ways of reading are constructed through the practices of literary criticism. Moreover, the contrast with 'ordinary language' signals the utilitarian framework which I discussed in chapter 2: poetry is distinguished from other kinds of relations between people and, consequently, from the power system whose pressures and limits ultimately determine those relations.

I attempted to control the metaphysical and transcendental implications of such a view of the art-work through linguistic analysis, but this tended again to reproduce the utilitarian framework, through the assumption of an alternative domain of 'science' of which linguistics was, or aspired to be, in possession. This tendency was further reinforced by that linguistics itself, which was based on Roman Jakobson's distinction between a referential and a poetic function in language, the latter manifested quintessentially in poetry, where 'poeticalness is not a supplementation of discourse with rhetorical adornment but a total re-evaluation of the discourse and of all its components whatsoever', effecting a 'conversion of a message into an enduring thing'.[2] Thus the theory, to which I was appealing for an alternative account to that of conventional criticism, already had inscribed within it the utilitarian distinction which I would now want to challenge.

In a way, I realized that I was identifying not so much properties of the poetry as a way of reading: 'It seems to be a fact about the way in which we perceive structures that once having discerned elements of a pattern we will naturally proceed to assimilate into it all relevant items in the context.'[3] This point is made decisively by Jonathan Culler in *Structuralist Poetics*, where he describes the perception of a high density of structuration as the specific reading experience of lyric poetry, and takes it to arise out of expectations which we bring to the reading of a poem – 'a set of conventions determining how the sequence is to be read'.[4] The criticism of Culler, nevertheless, and of that kind of structuralism (he invokes Greimas, Todorov and some work of Barthes – p. 172), is that it is content to stop there, when it has established what the reading conventions are, rather than pursue their political implications through an analysis of their constitution in history. Thus Culler also remains within the utilitarian framework, leaving unchallenged the idea that 'Poetry lies at the centre of the literary experience because it is the form that most clearly asserts the specificity of literature, its difference from ordinary discourse by an empirical individual about the world' (*Structuralist Poetics*, p. 162).

At the same time, the idea that poetry is densely

structured language derives from the Romantics (as Culler points out – p. 171), and was consolidated during the Victorian period. Palgrave chose his lyrics for the *Golden Treasury* on the principle, 'above all, that excellence should be looked for rather in the whole than in the parts' and omitted passages 'only when the piece could be thus brought to a closer lyrical unity' (p. viii). Consequently we may assume that Tennyson composed *with this in mind*, and therefore that many of his short poems may indeed manifest it. '"Every short poem", he remarked, "should have a definite shape, like the curve, sometimes a single, sometimes a double one, assumed by a severed tress or the rind of an apple when flung on the floor"' (*Memoir*, p. 871). At this point it becomes difficult to distinguish the properties of the poem from the conventions of reading, since both are constructed within the same discourse. This fact does not give us what many structuralists have looked for, namely an exclusive definition of poetry, nor does it justify the privileges accorded to poetic language in conventional criticism. Nevertheless, the kind of structural density which Tennyson deploys is one of several features of his writing which invites attention.

This song is read to herself by Ida in *The Princess* at the point where she is reconsidering her rejection of the prince's suit:

> Now sleeps the crimson petal, now the white;
> Nor waves the cypress in the palace walk;
> Nor winks the gold fin in the porphyry font:
> The fire-fly wakens: waken thou with me.
>
> Now droops the milkwhite peacock like a ghost,
> And like a ghost she glimmers on to me.
>
> Now lies the Earth all Danaë to the stars,
> And all thy heart lies open unto me.
>
> Now slides the silent meteor on, and leaves
> A shining furrow, as thy thoughts in me.

> Now folds the lily all her sweetness up,
> And slips into the bosom of the lake:
> So fold thyself, my dearest, thou, and slip
> Into my bosom and be lost in me.

There is an obvious shape to this poem. Syntactical structures are in parallel both within and between the divisions marked by the arrangement of the lines, and they point to a systematic relationship between natural objects or creatures and the movements of the two lovers, as well as to a sequence in those movements. The structural density admired by Palgrave and Tennyson lies within this shape, in the teasing interplay between positive and negative connections and active and passive roles. The structure is not simple: it arises through an alternation of correspondences and differences which builds only gradually, and with work from the reader, towards a complex outcome.

In the first line, the repeated 'now' may signify either intensity of the present (in this one moment, now) or alternation (at this moment the crimson, at that the white). This uncertain effect is developed into the next two lines by the relationship between 'now' and 'nor': they sound alike but, logically, they are establishing a contrast; yet the contrast is finally a similarity, since the idea in all the first three lines is of absence of movement. And in the fourth line the woman, 'thou', is both like the still features in that she is asleep, and like the fire-fly in that she is to waken. The effect is sustained in lines 5–6, for the peacock seems to be like the lady (both are 'like a ghost') but 'glimmers on to me' sounds more active than 'droops' ('glimmers on' at first seems passive and stationary – she continues to glimmer – but then 'on' becomes 'on to', suggesting movement). Lines 7–10 introduce another model of divergence/convergence: they take us outwards to vastly more distant objects of analogy and inwards to the lovers' consciousness. At the same time, there is a movement of interchange, for whilst the speaker enters the heart of the lady (as Jove's golden rain entered Danaë), it is the lady who corresponds to the meteor, her thoughts which enter the speaker.

This interchange in lines 7–10 proves to be a change of direction and the pivot of the poem, for it establishes the lady as the active one. Although the speaker exhorted her to wake and her heart lies open to him, her thoughts move like a meteor and in the final lines she is like the lily which folds her sweetness up and slips into the lake. This casting of the lady in the active role is relevant to *The Princess*, where (as I remark in the next chapter) conventionally 'feminine' qualities are attributed to the prince. To the modern reader at least, it may seem that implicitly phallic imagery is deployed in a direction which is the opposite of the customary one: it is the lady who 'slips into' the male speaker. Yet despite the lady's active role, the outcome is that the male speaker, without moving, has absorbed her. She began the poem in a state of solitary oblivion, analogous to isolated natural phenomena; she ends it in oblivion once more, 'lost in me', with all her activity used in the process of her incorporation into the man. The indeterminacy – which offers structures, then denies them, and then offers them more complexly – suggests the hesitancy and the final success of the speaker's wooing. Every detail seems to be working so much harder, more purposefully, than in 'ordinary' language.

The quest of structuralist criticism for a systematic density of implication is met by the manifest and self-conscious organization of 'Now sleeps the crimson petal'. Critics have asserted comparable levels of organization in long poems like the Arthurian idylls: J. M. Gray points in 'Balin and Balan' to 'dramatic parallelism, multi-levelled implication and symbolic analogy. . . . By such the poem has an *inner* coherence'.[5] However, this is by no means the sole tendency in Tennyson's writing: it is challenged by the use of conventionally 'poetic' effects apparently for their own sake. In *Idylls of the King*, certainly, the structures which critics have discerned coexist with a powerful countervailing tendency towards dispersal into local effects. Even in 'Now sleeps the crimson petal' it is doubtful how far the intricate patterning of sound can be demonstrated as contributing to a unified whole. With this thought in mind,

Northrop Frye quotes from 'Oenone' and observes: 'the repetitions in Tennyson slow down the advance of ideas and narrative, compel the rhythm to return on itself, and elaborate what is essentially a pattern of varied and contrasting sound';[6] and E. L. Epstein quotes from 'Tithonus' to find that 'the vowel patterning seems to operate on its own, and even tends to de-emphasize the specific message.'[7] This tendency towards a self-sufficient sound patterning is finally at odds with a demand for complete structural integration: the effect is there to make the language more dense *in itself* rather than to build towards a significant structure. The underlying conception is illustrated by Tennyson himself when he remarks of *The Princess*: 'In defence of what some have called the too poetical passages, it should be recollected that the poet of the party was requested to "dress the tale up poetically".'[8] Such 'dressing up' pulls against the idea of a structured totality; nevertheless, I will argue in a moment that both tendencies may be viewed as part of the same larger project.

Within the framework I was using in *The Language of Tennyson's 'In Memoriam'*, I had some difficulty in handling the charge that 'Tennyson sought,by disguising his meaning in vague or ornate diction, to give his writing a merely artificial elevation' (p. 44). I now think that Tennyson cannot be 'defended' on this score, though I would want to consider what is really going on, rather than merely prefer one mode against another. The complaint goes back at least to Walter Bagehot, who responded to the publication of *Enoch Arden* in 1864 with a review which distinguished pure, ornate and grotesque poetry. Wordsworth and Milton are taken as instances of the first, Browning of the third. Ornate poetry is instanced by Tennyson and is defined thus: 'The essence of ornate art is . . . to accumulate round the typical object, everything which can be said about it, every associated thought that can be connected with it, without impairing the essence of the delineation.'[9]

Bagehot quotes the description of the tropical island upon which Enoch is wrecked:

A shipwrecked sailor, waiting for a sail:
No sail from day to day, but every day
The sunrise broken into scarlet shafts
Among the palms and ferns and precipices;
The blaze upon the waters to the east;
The blaze upon his island overhead;
The blaze upon the waters to the west;
Then the great stars that globed themselves in Heaven,
The hollower-bellowing ocean, and again
The scarlet shafts of sunrise – but no sail.

(lines 586–95)

The passage manifests structural correspondences such as I discussed in 'Now sleeps the crimson petal', but tends more towards an accumulation of effect than the delicate distinctions of that poem; Bagehot identifies 'a mist of beauty, an excess of fascination, a complication of charm' (p. 355). Within the principle that the poem should be a highly structured totality, such elaborate writing has to be defended as relevant to the whole effect. Bagehot denies that it is, declaring that there is 'a great deal . . . which a rough sailor like Enoch Arden certainly would not have perceived' (p. 352). A reply is offered by Martin Dodsworth: 'Tennyson's point, which Bagehot misses, is that Enoch *feels* nothing of the splendours described; his attention is turned completely away from them.'[10] This is fair but, as Dodsworth actually suggests, it is not quite enough: he says that the repetitions of words and phrases and accumulations of physical detail in the passage 'are dramatically appropriate to the subject-matter', but also that 'the style is consistently Tennysonian' and the subject-matter 'highly characteristic of the poet' (p. 12). There is a distinctively Tennysonian excess in the language, which goes beyond the 'appropriate'.

The second passage Bagehot quotes is even more difficult to deal with within the canons of structural relevance:

> Enoch's white horse, and Enoch's ocean-spoil
> In ocean-smelling osier, and his face,
> Rough-reddened with a thousand winter gales,
> Not only to the market-cross were known,
> But in the leafy lanes behind the down,
> Far as the portal-warding lion-whelp,
> And peacock-yewtree of the lonely Hall,
> Whose Friday fare was Enoch's ministering.
>
> (lines 93–100)

The reader may have trouble working out that this is all about the fact that Enoch sells fish in the market and also supplies the upper classes. Here we are plainly dealing with a stylistic mannerism. Bagehot's analysis is rather limited:

> Many of the characters of real life, if brought distinctly, prominently, and plainly before the mind, as they really are, if shown in their inner nature, their actual essence, are doubtless very unpleasant. They would be horrid to meet and horrid to think of. We fear it must be owned that Enoch Arden is this kind of person. A dirty sailor who did *not* go home to his wife is not an agreeable being: a varnish must be put on him to make him shine. (p. 363)

What Bagehot does not remark is that all sorts of Tennysonian characters are treated in the same way as Enoch; he is actually saying that the manner seems to him absurd when applied to a lower-class person. The point is that Tennyson believed such 'dressing up' proper to poetry, and it has little to do with structural relevance.

What Tennyson cannot be accused of – and the point comprises both ornateness and structural density – is transparency of style. Bagehot attributes transparency to 'pure' poetry: 'The form is sometimes said to be bare, the accessories are sometimes said to be invisible, because the appendages are so choice that the shape only is perceived'

(p. 342); so 'to Wordsworth has been vouchsafed the last grace of the self-denying artist; you think neither of him nor his style, but you cannot help thinking of – you *must* recall – the exact phrase, the *very* sentiment he wished' (p.345). As Antony Easthope has pointed out, this Wordsworthian effect sets aside the whole preceding rhetorical tradition in English poetry. In the Preface to *Lyrical Ballads*, Wordsworth maintains that poetry is 'so wholly transparent to experience that it is virtually identical with it', and in the 1802 Appendix to the Preface he 'gives a polemical history of rhetoric as the "mechanical adoption" of "figures of speech", "a motley masquerade of tricks, quaintnesses, hieroglyphics, and enigmas"'.[11] Such an attempt to efface the process of writing is one way of trying to get past the fact that experience is always constructed in language; a transparent style seems to assert a direct access to reality.

I discussed in chapter 3 Tennyson's yearning to locate an ultimate ground of being and truth beyond language, attributing it both to personal anxiety and to the disorienting political conditions in which poetry was expected to find a role for itself. In Derrida's terms, Tennyson strives within the tradition of western metaphysics to bridge or eradicate the gap between language and reality. One way of pursuing this always-postponed goal is to make language transparent. Richard Rorty has observed that this has been a typical strategy of philosophers, who seem to 'think that writing is a means of representing facts, and that the more "written" writing is – the less transparent to what it represents and the more concerned with its relation to others' writings – the worse it must be'.[12] Tennyson takes an opposite path: he seeks to make his language as dense and substantial as possible. It might be argued, as Easthope does of Modernist poetry, that 'by insisting on itself as production it asserts the subject as made, constituted, relative rather than absolute' (*Poetry as Discourse*, p. 135): that such self-conscious linguistic excess draws attention to the constructedness of what we imagine to be reality. But although Tennyson's verse may be read to this effect (which, indirectly, is what I am doing), to suggest that this was in some sense his project would be to ignore all the other indications that Tennyson wanted desperately to assert an ultimate reality, and to discover a means of apprehending it through poetic language. It seems, rather, that both the structural density and the ornateness which Tennyson cultivated are parts of his strategy for limiting the arbitrariness of the sign and imparting a sense of presence. The elaborate diction, the obtrusive syntax and the intense effects of sound and rhythm all act in the same direction. They offer not an enhanced transparency in the relationship between sign and referent, but an unattributed density *in the sign itself*.

Rather than closing the gap between sign and referent, Tennyson creates, as it were, a plenitude of the sign. Language cannot be brought closer to the world, but it can be made more full and substantial *in itself*. In Tennyson's writing any particular word has, or appears to have, many reasons for being appropriate: it is linked to other words through effects of sound and rhythm, syntactical parallelism, and figurative associations which may extend through a network of images across hundreds of lines; and passages which seem ornate rather than organic also seem to make the word more substantial in itself. Thus the arbitrariness of language seems to be controlled. And it all works in relative independence of reference to the world: significance begins to seem a property of the poem, not of the world. The poem creates an alternative reality which is bounded entirely by its language. Of course a deception, no doubt benign, is involved here: for if the relationship between sign and referent is in principle arbitrary, then to multiply the facets of that relationship will not help. Twenty kinds of arbitrary relationship, however much they interlock, are still arbitrary. There is – can be – only the *impression* of plenitude. Perhaps the distinction between highly structured and ornate poetry amounts to that between those passages where we find this impression achieved, and those where we do not. Through this strategy of 'filling up' the sign, Tennyson sought to locate a ground of truth and ultimate being beyond the unstable constructions of language.

Tennyson's early awareness that the sign lacks the fulness of the real world is powerfully expressed in 'Early Spring', a poem written in 1833 but published only in 1883 and without most of the stanzas I will discuss. The poem celebrates the marvellous budding forth of spring, and after twenty-eight lines of evocative description the idea of language enters:

> My tricksy fancies range,
>   And, lightly stirred,
> Ring little bells of change
>   From word to word.

But this thought of correspondence between words and reality provokes Tennyson, immediately, to address its inadequacy:

> Ah! lightest words are lead,
>   Gross to make plain
> Myriads of hints of things
>   That orb and wane.

The poem is forced away from description and into abstraction:

> O fullness of the worlds!
>   O termless field,
> Relation, difference,
>   Not all concealed,
> Fair feast of every sense
>   In part revealed.

The world has a fulness beyond that of language: it is 'termless', not subject to the confines of language. The endless possibilities of meaning in the world – all its relatedness and distinctions – are there, not narrowed into the structures of language but laid out before the viewer. Yet there is a lack: it is '*Not all* concealed . . . *In part* revealed'. The limits of language are, after all, in some measure the limits of consciousness. We may regard this as an acknowledgement of the extent to which consciousness is constructed in language – we see that which language encourages or permits us to see. More likely, Tennyson means that there is a spiritual implication in the landscape which is only partially appreciated through the senses, for the last stanza reads:

> O soul reflecting forms
>   Of this wide beach,
> Comparing at thy will
>   Each form with each,
> Let tears of wonder fill
>   Thy void of speech.

The language here struggles to relate the fullness of the landscape to that of the soul: the lack of a clear grammatical subject for the second two lines enacts Tennyson's difficulty in locating a perceiving self which is free from the inhibitions of language, which can compare 'at . . . will'. The void which speech opens up can be filled only by tears; it is a question for interpretive license whether we should remark that the tears will interrupt the poet's view, making his experience increasingly self-constructed. In 1883 Tennyson withdrew these awkward implications and offered a final stanza which returns to the 'Heavenly Power' of the poem's opening:[13]

> For now the Heavenly Power
>   Makes all things new,
> And thaws the cold, and fills
>   The flower with dew;
> The blackbirds have their wills,
>   The poets too.

The last line is new. It asserts the poet's harmony with the external world and his achievement, presumably poetic achievement: he has done what he wills, and the poem is finished. A proclamation of success replaces the intensifying problematization of the early version.

That in poetry the defect of words is remedied seems to have been Tennyson's customary assumption (though he would still, as I instanced in chapter 3, suggest that visionary moments are beyond all language). Hence his emphasis when he wrote to Emily Sellwood in 1839: 'In *letters*, words too often prove a bar of hindrance instead of a bond of union'.[14] Poetry affords a special fulness of significance. Tennyson's view here converges upon a whole movement in European poetry. Gérard Genette finds that for Mallarmé 'the nonmimetic character of language' – its general failure to give transparent access to a secure referent in reality – is 'the opportunity and the condition for poetry to exist', for poetry is the special mode of language which compensates for 'the defect of languages'.[15] Genette uses the term 'Cratylism' (from Plato via Barthes) for 'that great secular myth which wants language to imitate ideas and, contrary to the precisions of linguistic science, wants signs to be motivated' (p. 360). The move of Mallarmé and Valéry, to create not a transparency of the sign but an incantatory, self-sufficient density of language, Genette calls 'secondary Cratylism' –

a Cratylism of the poem. . . . Henceforth there are two languages in language, one of which (everyday language) is left to arbitrariness and convention, while the other (poetic language) is the refuge of mimetic virtue, the locus of the miraculous survival of the primitive verb in all its 'incantatory' power. (p. 363)

As I noted at the end of chapter 2, Genette locates this position within a utilitarian framework such as I have identified.

Hence the cultivation, apparently for their own sake, of 'musical' properties in verse. Valéry's key statement, Genette points out, is that 'the power of verse stems from an *indefinable* harmony between what it *says* and what it *is*' (p. 366): 'music' is needed for its suggestiveness. All this is anticipated in Hallam's review of *Poems, Chiefly Lyrical*, in which he says that great poets like Dante and Petrarch

> produce two-thirds of their effect by *sound*. Not that
> they sacrifice sense to sound, but that sound conveys
> their meaning, where words would not. There are
> innumerable shades of fine emotion in the human
> heart, especially when the senses are keen and
> vigilant, which are too subtle and too rapid to admit of
> corresponding phrases. The understanding takes no
> definite note of them; how then can they leave
> signatures in language? Yet they exist; in plenitude of
> being and beauty they exist; and in music they find a
> medium through which they pass from heart to heart.
> (Armstrong, pp. 96–7)

It is all there: the fullness of experience, especially the poet's experience, the inadequacy of ordinary language, the short-circuiting of the usual modes of reference to the world, and the achievement of a marvellously direct communication 'from heart to heart'.

As well as intoning his own name, Tennyson found a strange charm in the words 'Far – Far – Away', and he wrote about it in 1888 in a poem called that:

> What vague world-whisper, mystic pain or joy,
> Through those three words would haunt him when a
> boy,
> > Far – far – away?
>
> A whisper from his dawn of life? a breath
> From some fair dawn beyond the doors of death
> > Far – far – away?
>
> Far, far, how far? from o'er the gates of Birth,
> The faint horizons, all the bounds of earth,
> > Far – far – away?
>
> What charm in words, a charm no words could give?
> O dying words, can Music make you live
> > Far – far – away?

This is a quintessential Tennyson poem: the repeating of the words so that language evaporates and points beyond itself to what the poet takes to be an intuition of an ultimate reality; the location of imaginative experience in remote places and the sense that the horizon recedes ('Far, far, how far?'); the suggestion that words cannot do that which nevertheless is being done by poetical magic. The poem is subtitled '(For Music)', suggesting both that the poem should be set to music because only thus could it fully transcend ordinary language, and that the poem is dedicated to music whose profound power is thus identified as that of the words 'Far – far – away', a power beyond their power as words. So in the last stanza we should understand 'charm' as magic, incantation: it is through the special power of music that these words may be made fully vital – because their effect was always more like that of music than ordinary language. A. Dwight Culler quotes R. E. Horne's comment: 'he will write you a poem with nothing in it except music, and as if its music were everything, it shall charm your soul.'[16]

That Literature generally, and poetry in particular, should attain to some such density of effect, constituting through and beyond language a reality which language cannot reach, became a commonplace of literary criticism as it developed within the utilitarian framework discussed in chapter 2. In *Mythologies*, Roland Barthes observes that poetry 'tries to transform the sign back into meaning: its ideal, ultimately, would be to reach not the meaning of words, but the meaning of things themselves. This is why it clouds the language, increases as much as it can the abstractness of the concept and the arbitrariness of the sign and stretches to the limit the link between signifier and signified.'[17] It is through this project – to which Tennyson contributed crucially – that poetry stakes its claim over against utilitarianism, political economy and machinery: it heals the breach between humankind and reality.

Symbol and Allegory

Such is the status of the idea of Literature as the one mode which restores a relationship between language and reality, that it has been customary to praise Tennyson in so far as he instantiated or anticipated the idea. This has been the dominant critical stance ever since Marshall McLuhan's essay of 1951, which offered 'Mariana' as proving that 'the most sophisticated symbolist poetry could be written fifty years before the Symbolists' – 'Syntax becomes music, as in Tennyson's "Mariana"'.[18] W. K. Wimsatt, Jr traced the symbolic mode to Romantic poetry, finding that there tenor and vehicle, the literal and figurative aspects of an image, 'are wrought in a parallel process out of the same material . . . the common feat of the romantic nature poets was to read meanings into the landscape'. Thus a Romantic metaphysic – 'of an animate, plastic nature, not transcending but immanent in and breathing through all things' – is embodied.[19] In other words, this kind of poetry has as its objective the bridging of the gap between consciousness and the world, the effacing of the constructing role of language. Wimsatt called his book *The Verbal Icon* because semioticians like Charles Peirce use the term 'icon' to refer to 'a verbal sign which *somehow* shares the properties of, or resembles, the objects which it denotes' (p. x). This Romantic poetry, Wimsatt believed, came close to symbolism (p. 116).

McLuhan also derived the symbolic mode from the Romantics, but a major goal of deconstructive criticism has been to reverse both the analysis and the preference. Paul de Man sees the priority of symbol over allegory in modern critical theory as a refusal 'to distinguish between experience and the representation of this experience', and disputes that such a priority is definitely present in the work of Wordsworth and Coleridge. In fact, when Wordsworth's poetry is fully authentic it renounces 'the seductiveness and the poetic resources of a symbolical diction':

> Whereas the symbol postulates the possibility of an identity or identification, allegory designates primarily a distance in relation to its own origin, and, renouncing the nostalgia and the desire to coincide, it establishes its language in the void of this temporal difference. In so doing, it prevents the self from an illusory identification with the non-self, which is now fully, though painfully, recognized as a non-self. It is this painful knowledge that we perceive at the moments when early romantic literature finds its true voice.[20]

We may be suspicious of the painful heroism of the stance proposed here: it is this which allows the existentialist recuperation of the poetic genius as trembling upon the brink of the impossible and yet eternally enticing achievement of full identity between sign and referent which I criticized in the criticism of Hartman in chapter 3. Nonetheless, de Man's thought is profound: it alleges that Wordsworth resisted the temptation to fill up the sign, that he sought a language which exposes rather than cultivates that temptation, and that subsequent writers lost this insight. (The relation between this analysis of Wordsworth's writing and Easthope's, referred to earlier, is beyond the scope of this book. Briefly, I think Easthope reads the manifest general tendency of Wordsworth's language whereas de Man probes for breaks in that tendency.) The modes of language I have identified so far in Tennyson's poetry would suggest that he did his best to cultivate the symbolic mode. Nevertheless, there are important questions to be considered.

R. H. Hutton in 1888 discussed 'Break, break, break' as a poem where Tennyson turns 'an ordinary sea-shore landscape into a means of finding a voice indescribably sweet for the dumb spirit of human loss'.[21] On this account, the poem is symbolic – it takes the opposite course from allegory in de Man's account, for his criterion is that 'it prevents the self from an illusory identification with the non-self.'[22] In another essay he observes: 'as long as we can distinguish between literal and figural meaning, we can translate the figure back to its proper referent.'[23] Unravelling the literal and the figurative is precisely what Tennyson makes difficult.

Break, break, break,
   On thy cold gray stones, O Sea!
And I would that my tongue could utter
   The thoughts that arise in me.

O well for the fisherman's boy,
   That he shouts with his sister at play!
O well for the sailor lad,
   That he sings in his boat on the bay!

And the stately ships go on
   To their haven under the hill;
But O for the touch of a vanished hand,
   And the sound of a voice that is still!

Break, break, break,
   At the foot of thy crags, O Sea!
But the tender grace of a day that is dead
   Will never come back to me.

The first two lines seem to apostrophize the sea but are followed by an intimation that there is something more which the poet would say: the literal is not allowed to stand as a satisfactory utterance. The second stanza pursues this sense: it is 'well for' other people but not, we presume, for the poet. The third stanza adds an image and then offers an explanation of the feeling which cannot be uttered, of the lack in the descriptions. The last stanza invites us explicitly to put the seascape and the poet's loss together, to read back the poet's state of mind into the descriptions. David Shaw offers such a reading:

The loneliness of the sea, the peace of the ships, the mysterious charm of the singing create a meaning to be apprehended only through the metaphors – a

significance always just out of sight and just beyond
definition. But there is also a kind of third-
dimensional significance, pointing from the breaking
waves to the mourner's breaking heart, and from the
sea that breaks at the foot of the crags to the boundless
deep beyond.[24]

Shaw adapts Wimsatt's point, in the paper I have
mentioned, about the children that 'sport upon the shore'
in Wordsworth's 'Intimations' ode: the fisherman's boy,
the sailor lad and the stately ships '"are not strictly parts of
the . . . vehicle". . . . Attracted to the vehicle, they are really
images of the soul.'[25] Literal and figurative cross over and
confound customary distinctions.

James J. Sherry, following suggestions of Christopher
Ricks, has argued that 'Break, break, break' resists such a
symbolic reading: his case rests on the 'disjunctions' which
occur as the poem moves between imagistic and discursive
writing. The 'Ands' in lines three and nine and the 'Buts' of
the third and fourth stanzas 'seem more like signs that we
should connect things than real connections. They remain
dissatisfying' and disrupt the symbolic mode.[26] However,
we might say, conversely, that the gap created by those
'Ands' and 'Buts' is precisely what demands the move
across from literal to figurative: it is that gap which the
reader is invited to fill by taking up the representation
symbolically. There is, of course, a disjunction between the
happy youngsters and the poet's state of loss, but that does
not disturb the symbolic mode. As with the faith/doubt
opposition I discussed in chapter 3, a failure of connection
does not deny the framework within which connection is
envisaged. The presence and the power of the symbolic
mode is confirmed by the credibility with which Shaw
develops more fundamental and remote associations across
the apparent divide between the poet and the seascape.

The fact is that the case may be made either way. The
'Ands' and 'Buts' can be held, with equal consistency,
either to demand symbolic reading or to expose that
demand, depending on the reader's preparedness to col-

laborate in the symbolist project – compare again chapter 3, where I remarked how the reader may either go along with intimations of ultimate reality in 'The Ancient Sage' or warily read through them, disclosing the strategies they deploy. De Man explains:

> The innumerable writings that dominate our lives are made intelligible by a preordained agreement as to their referential authority; this agreement however is merely contractual, never constitutive. It can be broken at all times and every piece of writing can be questioned as to its rhetorical mode.[27]

How far any particular strategy of poetic language carries conviction or exposes its own construction is bound to be a matter of interpretive license. The poem is within the symbolic mode, but is not an unchallengable instance of it; indeed, there can be no such instance.

Another example. 'Mariana' is obviously related to the symbolist project. Mill put the point precisely when he singled it out as exemplifying Tennyson's 'power of *creating* scenery, in keeping with some state of human feeling; so fitted to it as to be the embodied symbol of it, and to summon up the state of feeling itself, with a force not to be surpassed by anything but reality'.[28] Here is the stanza which perhaps offers the largest opportunity for allegorical reading:

> Her tears fell with the dews at even;
>   Her tears fell ere the dews were dried;
> She could not look on the sweet heaven,
>   Either at morn or eventide.
> After the flitting of the bats,
>   When thickest dark did trance the sky,
>   She drew her casement-curtain by,
> And glanced athwart the glooming flats.
>   She only said, 'The night is dreary,
>   He cometh not', she said;
>   She said, 'I am aweary, aweary,
>   I would that I were dead!'

Here Sherry is able to point out that 'sweet heaven' (line 3) is not the view of Mariana's consciousness. There is within the poem another perspective on the landscape, and this undercuts the identification of self with non-self: 'As soon as we become aware of a difference, a discrepancy, Mariana's reading of the world no longer seems to inhere in its very structure but to be imposed from without upon objects which have meanings of their own.'[29] And Sherry adds, again following Ricks, that our awareness of the ending of *Measure for Measure* further undermines the authenticity of Mariana's investment of self in the world; and he believes that 'trance' (in the sixth line quoted) suggests Mariana's 'coercion of the world to conform to her despair'. So we are 'brought to realize the essentially allegorical nature of all interpretation' (pp. 213–4).

I would say, again, that the reader has scope here for divergent readings. The complexity arises, basically, from the fact of narration: it is the narrative voice which is potentially separate from Mariana, and which (in the title and the epigraph) knows of *Measure for Measure* (I will say more of this shortly). Nevertheless, the narrator seems equally committed to the identification of self and non-self, for it is he (?she) who says the heaven is 'sweet', offering not a literal representation but an emotional and evaluative investment, alternative to but in the same mode as Mariana's. Nor is there reason to think that the narrator dissociates himself from the idea that 'thickest dark did trance the sky' – that is offered without a hint of distantiation. The consciousness of Mariana is disturbed in its relation with the landscape, but not by a fundamentally different mode of seeing. The deconstructive reading is there, perhaps, for the reader determined to read for gaps and incoherences rather than for achieved effects, but the poem hardly insists upon it.

That is it possible to discern breaks in the links between consciousness, language and the world does not mean that Tennyson is a deconstructionist before his time. To suppose that is to evade what is radical about deconstruction, as initiated by Derrida – namely that it knows that it is less a philosophical standpoint (with which Tennyson, for instance, may accord or otherwise) than *a way of reading*. While it is reasonable to assert, as de Man does, though perhaps too sedulously, that certain texts seem positively to instigate such a reading, *any* text may be read with an eye for its complicity in the notion that language affords access to an ultimate reality, and for breaks which expose the delusory nature of that notion. For the attempt to fill up the sign *must always be questionable*. As de Man concludes, the 'symbolical style will never be allowed to exist in serenity; since it is a veil thrown over a light one no longer wishes to perceive, it will never be able to gain an entirely good poetic conscience'.[30] So the fact that Tennyson's poetry can be deconstructed does not mean that he is to be recruited as a deconstructionist. On the contrary, it is the attempt to fuse mind and object through the medium of language which affords the opportunity for disclosing that attempt to be forced.

The Absent Other

Because it is always impossible to fill up the sign, the attempt is very likely to be shot through with a sense of loss and absence. Derrida affirms: 'There will be no unique name, not even the name of Being. It must be conceived without *nostalgia*.'[31] But even here there is a hint of stoicism which (I have suggested) becomes a renewed romantic yearning in Hartman and even de Man. In Tennyson loss and absence are pervasive.

In the terms of Lacanian psychoanalysis the attempt to fill up language is an attempt to regain the realm of the imaginary – the condition characterized by a sense of ideal harmony and wholeness which precedes the entrance into language and identity. I discussed in chapter 3 how Tennyson's 'waking trances' may be regarded as a projection on to a supposed ultimate reality of that ideal harmony and wholeness; how 'The Lady of Shalott', 'Supposed Confessions', *The Princess* and *In Memoriam* (45) witness to a preoccupation with the infant's move into language and identity, veering away from the discovery that the self is a construction which is always in language, and casting around for an ultimate reality somehow beyond language. The attempt to fill up the sign is also a quest for the imaginary, where the 'I' is the entire centre of its own world, others seem simply extensions or further versions of it, and language seems to offer some full relation between word and thing. Anthony Wilden explains:

> Lacan would view the newborn child as an 'absolute subject' in a totally intransitive relationship to the world he cannot yet distinguish from himself. For the object to be discovered by the child it must be *absent*. At the psychological level the partial object conveys the lack which creates the desire for unity from which the movement toward identification springs – since identification is itself dependent upon the discovery of *difference*, itself a kind of absence. At the logical or epistemological level, says Lacan, the 'lack of object' is the gap in the signifying chain which the subject seeks to fill at the level of the signifier.[32]

The very process of discovering the world to be other than the self, therefore, is dependent on a sense of absence, and this runs through language, which begins with the task of designating the absent other. The retrieval of this initial and fundamental loss is the impossible project of 'Mariana' and 'Break, break, break'. Tennyson virtually intuits as much in 'Far – Far – Away', when he speculates on the source of the 'vague world-whisper' which he hears through 'those three words' –

> A whisper from the dawn of life? a breath
> From some fair dawn beyond the doors of death
>   Far – far – away?

It is indeed 'a charm no words could give'.

Most commentators remark the importance of loss as a theme in Tennyson's work.[33] In fact, most of his most powerful poems which aspire to remedy the defect of language by investing the world with consciousness have personal loss as their theme. T. S. Eliot put the two together when summing up Tennyson's achievement, though without quite articulating a link between them: 'Tennyson is the great master of metric as well as of melancholia; I do not think any poet in English has ever had a finer ear for vowel sound, as well as subtler feeling for some moods of anguish'.[34] This conjunction of theme and technique works so well for Tennyson, I suggest, because the two have a common origin and structure. The point at which the infant moves into language and identity is constitutive also of desire for another person (until that point the other person, theorized in psychoanalysis as the mother, is not perceived as other, as an object of desire). This also is, necessarily, accompanied by a sense of loss:

> desire itself, and with it, sexual desire, can only exist by virtue of its alienation . . . the object that is longed for only comes into existence *as an object* when it is lost to the baby or infant. . . . The baby's need can be met, its demand responded to, but its desire only exists because of the initial failure of satisfaction. Desire persists as an effect of a primordial absence and it therefore indicates that, in this area, there is something fundamentally impossible about satisfaction itself.[35]

The other person is desired, just like the fully motivated sign, to restore the imaginary wholeness, but this demand is equally impossible of fulfilment: there is no ultimate other, no final ground of being and meaning.

The appeal of the theme of loss for Tennyson obviously derives from particular personal needs, but the strength of many of his poems derives from their implication in a common human experience, and from the profound convergence within that experience of psychological, epistemological and linguistic factors. The sense of loss in Tennyson's symbolic poems – in 'Break, break, break', 'Mariana' and so much of his most characteristic work – is therefore doubly determined: the aspiration to fill up the sign coincides with the aspiration to fix the self securely through another person. Both originate in the same deprivation as the individual enters language and identity; both are imbued, necessarily, with the same sense of loss and absence. Indeed, we may say that these poems of yearning for personal and symbolic wholeness were triply determined, for they were produced within a construction of Literature which exiled the poet from central human concerns to margins of experience.

Tennyson wrote 'In the Valley of Cauteretz' in 1861 when he revisited the Pyrenean valley where he had been with Arthur Hallam in 1830:

> All along the valley, stream that flashest white,
> Deepening thy voice with the deepening of the night,
> All along the valley, where thy waters flow,
> I walked with one I loved two and thirty years ago.
> All along the valley, while I walked today,
> The two and thirty years were a mist that rolls away;
> For all along the valley, down thy rocky bed,
> Thy living voice to me was as the voice of the dead,
> And all along the valley, by rock and cave and tree,
> The voice of the dead was a living voice to me.

Initially the stream is addressed as itself, but already in the second line there is a suggestion of 'deeper' meaning, and in the third the repetition of the opening phrase begins to develop an incantatory mood which seems to correspond to the reminiscence of the fourth line. This is the strategy of 'Break, break, break'. The second sentence (lines 5–10) seeks to close and repudiate the gap between human experience and the world through a characteristically dense handling of language. The thirty two years are redesignated in terms of landscape as 'a mist that rolls away', and then the stream's 'voice' is said to be 'living' (activating the personification which was in 'voice' as early as line 2) 'as the voice of the dead'. Consciousness and the world are involved with each other, so why not reverse the model? So Tennyson claims, finally, that 'The voice of the dead was a living voice to me.'

'In the Valley of Cauteretz' may be read as an affirmation of our one life with the dead, a witness achieved through the magical power of poetical language. But it may also be read, more persuasively I think, as manifesting the failure of language which, despite its lyric power, does not bring Hallam back to life. There is something willed about the repeated phrases and the inversion of the voices of the stream and Hallam: they are attempting to recover the irrecoverable, and even in the last line 'The voice of the dead' remains just that. For all the concluding assertion, it is a poem of loss and melancholy. As Kerry McSweeney puts it, 'the sober colouring' of the landscape 'is taken from the eye of a poet who has kept watch on his own mortality and pondered that of his beloved friend for almost three decades'.[36] This is the special Tennysonian melancholy: the loss of the imaginary wholeness which he associates with the loss of a loved person coincides with the inability of language quite to restore the imaginary wholeness.

Who is Speaking?

Although I have argued that the breaks which criticism is able to discern in Tennyson's symbolic mode are an inevitable feature of that mode, there is a systematic factor in his poems which undermines the attempt to fill up the sign. This is Tennyson's tendency to use narrators and dramatic speakers. I acknowledged earlier that the placing of Mariana's consciousness by the presence of a narrator, even though his attitude is hardly distinguishable from hers, inhibits the reader's sense that her consciousness, language and the world are in a full and necessary continuum.

> She only said, 'The night is dreary,
>   He cometh not', she said;
> She said, 'I am aweary, aweary,
>   I would that I were dead!'

'She said' interposes a frame, sets Mariana and her world apart as a narrative effect. And consider 'She only said': there are other things which she might have said, and they are known to the narrator. 'The Lady of Shalott' also has a veil of narrative between the Lady and the world which evokes her consciousness.

> But who hath seen her wave her hand?
> Or at the casement seen her stand?
> Or is she known in all the land,
>   The Lady of Shalott?

> (lines 24–7)

Such questions suggest other positions, other consciousnesses than the Lady's. There is a similar tendency in poems set in a framework, like 'The Lotos-Eaters', 'The Palace of Art' and 'Morte d'Arthur'.

De Man shows in 'The rhetoric of temporality' that commentators on the Romantics have persistent difficulty in deciding whether the impetus of the symbolic mode is fundamentally subjective or objective. In his view such 'ambivalences derived from an illusionary priority of a subject that had, in fact, to borrow from the outside world a temporal stability which it lacked within itself'.[37] The coherence of the human subject, whether apparently originating or perceiving, is essential to the mode. So Dwight Culler suggests that 'although the grange is described by the poetic speaker, only the refrain being put into Mariana's mouth, one has the impression that the entire poem is spoken by Mariana.' The narrator must be suppressed if the aim of the poem is taken to be 'realizing a state of consciousness'.[38] And hence the wish of admirers of *Idylls of the King* to assimilate that narrative to the symbolic mode. John D. Rosenberg writes: 'Tennyson creates an inclusive psychological landscape in which all the separate consciousnesses in the poem participate'; and J. M. Gray writes of Balin: 'In fact all the characters that appear to him in the woods are but his spectral doubles. In this sense he originates nearly everything that happens in the Idyll. It is his inner story.'[39]

Several of the poems where Tennyson cultivates most intensely the interpenetration of consciousness and landscape are dramatic monologues: thus he combines the symbolic mode, challengingly, with a disturbance of the poetic voice which we might expect to be its validating point of origin. 'Tithonus' is an instance.

> The woods decay, the woods decay and fall,
> The vapours weep their burthen to the ground,
> Man comes and tills the field and lies beneath,
> And after many a summer dies the swan.
> Me only cruel immortality
> Consumes: I wither slowly in thine arms,
> Here at the quiet limit of the world,
> A white-haired shadow roaming like a dream
> The ever-silent spaces of the East,
> Far-folded mists, and gleaming halls of morn.
>
> (lines 1–10)

These lines effect the full Tennysonian battery of techniques for making the sign appear motivated – description saturated with consciousness, incantatory repetitions and rhythms, all the resources of poetic language patterned so as to communicate a feeling of human mortality and, beyond that, the profound world-weariness which coincides so often in Tennyson with the symbolic mode. The first four lines we might well take to be general lyric comment on human life, such as Romantic poetry often offers in the first person – the thought and imagery are reminiscent of *The Prelude*, VI, 624–5: 'The immeasurable height/Of woods decaying, never to be decayed.' But lines 5–10 introduce the speaker and we recognize that he is not the poet in his own (supposed) person. The poem's title is 'Tithonus' and we see that the speaker is the mythical figure, doomed to immortal life but not immortal youth, the lover of the dawn whom he can no longer satisfy. This knowledge is important to our perception of Tithonus, for as with Mariana it gives a larger context for the story. When he wonders if it be true that 'The Gods themselves cannot recall their gifts' (line 49), we know that this is so, that Tithonus could not die and that he was released only by being turned into a grasshopper. Such knowledge places us in complicity with the organizing poet as against the speaker, limiting crucially the authority of the speaker and thus of the fulness of his language.

'Tithonus', like other dramatic monologues, has the rhetorical mode of a first-person lyric but a manifestly fictional speaker: it hovers between first-person and third-person, allowing the reader to settle confidently into neither. We cannot assume the direct expression which, since the Romantics, is generally signalled by the use of 'I' in a poem, but nor can we assume the authorial distantiation implied in narrative and drama. I have suggested elsewhere, following a suggestion of Käte Hamburger, that dramatic monologue occupies a special position between the lyric and the dramatic, it *feigns*: an invented speaker masquerades in the first person which customarily signifies the poet's voice.[40]

Criticism has experienced difficulty in handling dramatic monologue because of the customary assumption that the individual author is the manifest and sufficient origin of the work of art. Raman Selden has pointed out how twentieth-century belief in Literature's 'special and even autonomous status' produced an emphasis upon 'the voices and personae constructed by the author' as distinct from 'the author's own personality'. Yet this was not allowed to encroach upon the authority of the author: 'Most critics in the 1950s and 1960s accepted the concept of persona but always upon the stated or unstated understanding that the author retained his status as an underlying "presence" as creator and source of his voices.'[41] The split between first-

and third-person voices in dramatic monologue corresponds to the two standard ways of propounding the
author's authority (directly, or as the master mind behind
dramatic characters). The refusal of dramatic monologue
to fit into either has proved an embarrassment, and
commentators have been tempted to resolve it one way or
the other.

The most influential account has been Robert Langbaum's, and he takes the form towards the dramatic,
holding that we react to the speaker as a character separate
from the poet. This still centres the poet, as the organizer of
a tension between sympathy and judgement. The speaker is
a vehicle through which the poet explores, with a historical
and psychological awareness, the different positions that
have been held by different people.[42] However, Langbaum's model instance is 'My Last Duchess' by Browning
and his preferred Tennysonian instance is 'St Simeon
Stylites'. In 'Tithonus', 'The Lotos-Eaters' and 'Ulysses' he
finds 'a certain life-weariness, a longing for rest through
oblivion' which is 'most characteristic of Tennyson' (p. 83):
in other words, these poems, being less plainly dramatic,
drift back towards lyric. So, in fact, it is common to read
'Tithonus' as a displaced version of Tennyson's own
distress after the death of Hallam. Ricks in his edition
quotes Mary Jane Donahue for a critical keynote: 'it is clear
that, in choosing the mask of Tithonus, Tennyson reached
out to two of the most basic symbols, those of love between
man and woman and the frustration of love by age, to
express the peculiar and individual nature of his own
emotional injury.'[43] Failing to substantiate its claim to the
dramatic category, the poem is assimilated instead to the
lyric. Of course, the process is admitted to be complex, but
then the capacity to handle and embody complexity is one
of the things for which the poet is admired. Both the
dramatic and the lyric resolutions tidy up the indeterminacy of feigning and refer it, safely, to the concept of the
individual author.

It would be rash to move from humanist criticism's

alternative recuperations of the challenge of dramatic monologue to a claim that Tennyson anticipated a post-structuralist awareness of the construction of the human subject in language. One of Barthes' formulations of the issue includes a warning:

> For classical metaphysics, there was no disadvantage in 'dividing' the person (Racine: '*J'ai deux-hommes en moi*'); quite the contrary, decked out in two opposing terms, the person advanced like a good paradigm (*high/low, flesh/spirit, heaven/earth*); the parties to the conflict were reconciled in the establishment of a meaning: the meaning of Man. This is why, when we speak today of a divided subject, it is never to acknowledge his simple contradictions, his double postulations, etc.; it is a *diffraction* which is intended, a dispersion of energy in which there remains neither a central core nor a structure of meaning: I am not contradictory, I am dispersed.[44]

Not all divisions of the person imply a radical critique of the essential self: often enough they are ways of elaborating that concept. 'Tithonus' may be read either as an exposition of anxiety about the constructedness of the self, or as falling into an ideal opposition whose resolution is Man. It is salutary to compare two such readings.

Tithonus is not just fictional, he is mythical – an idea, perhaps, rather than a person. The feigning of the 'I' figure may be developed into a post-structuralist doubt about whether there is a human subject there at all. Tithonus' words encourage this doubt – he is a shadow, like a dream, 'once a man' (line 11); no longer in the world but 'at the quiet limit' (7), having varied 'from the kindly race of man' and passed 'beyond the goal of ordinance/Where all should pause' (28–31). Certainly the continuity of subjectivity is questioned:

> Ay me! ay me! with what another heart
> In days far-off, and with what other eyes

I used to watch – if I be he that watched –
The lucid outline forming round thee.

(lines 50–3)

Tithonus has difficulty in thinking of himself as a continuous person. He is unable to assert a personal,
psychological time in the face of his proximity to the dawn
which both determines and manifests, daily, a time by
which he is constructed: 'thy strong Hours indignant
worked their wills' (18). In terms of space, this effect
penetrates the structure of the poem's language. In
symbolic writing the world is invested with consciousness
to the point where the boundary between it and the human
subject is difficult to discern. In 'Tithonus' this process is
pushed one stage further, for although the dawn does not
cease to be a physical occurrence in the world, it is also a
personage, the mythical figure Eos.

Thy cheek begins to redden through the gloom,
Thy sweet eyes brighten slowly close to mine,
Ere yet they blind the stars, and the wild team
Which love thee, yearning for thy yoke, arise,
And shake the darkness from their loosened manes,
And beat the twilight into flakes of fire.

(lines 37–42)

Looked at one way, this passage seems to project human
feelings, presumably the speaker's, on to the dawn. Looked
at another way, the feelings are projected by the dawn, Eos,
on to Tithonus, and he is unable to respond adequately.
The blurring of literal and figurative, characteristic of
Tennyson's writing in the symbolic mode, tilts beyond the
point of balance so that individual subjectivity appears not
as the source of meaning in the world but as constructed *by*
the world. And this was so even 'In days far off':

[I] felt my blood
Glow with the glow that slowly crimsoned all
Thy presence and thy portals, while I lay,
Mouth, forehead, eyelids, growing dewy-warm.

(lines 55–8)

The glow in his blood was the glow of dawn, the dewy warmth was that of the sun on the landscape. Tithonus is an effect of his positioning in time and space. The scenery which in symbolic poetry supports the idea of individual consciousness here reacts back upon it with determining force.

So we may read a post-structuralist 'Tithonus', taking the feigning of dramatic monologue as a cue promoting perception of the instability of subjectivity. But the poem is also manifestly available to recuperative readings, which gather its terms into oppositions in which, as Barthes suggests, one pole governs the other and conflict is dissolved into allegedly universal verities. Raman Selden proposes that Beckett's *Krapp's Last Tape*, by insisting on 'discontinuity between old and new self . . . places a question mark over the ontological standing of the "self"'. This is quite like my post-structuralist reading of 'Tithonus', with the tape recordings of the previous selves endlessly returning like the dawn to confront subjectivity with the evidence of its own constructedness. But, Selden points out, the play can also be read to disclose an emergent affirmation, as it is by Peter Brook, for whom Beckett 'forges his merciless "no" out of a longing for "yes"'.[45] So in David Shaw's account of 'Tithonus', 'though the speaker's main craving has been for immortality, it has always been qualified by a contradictory desire for immediacy and warmth, which carry with them the penalty of death.'[46] Tithonus is unable to choose decisively between these two desires, and Shaw elaborates the uncertain direction characteristic of the speaker in the Langbaum view of dramatic monologue. Nevertheless, there *is* a resolution – located, of course, in the presiding genius of Tennyson: 'Honestly recording what he finds, Tennyson can leave Tithonus – and the reader, too – to discover for themselves the harsh but consoling truth that whoever rightly understands and celebrates death, at the same time magnifies life' (Shaw, p. 93).

Even while allowing the possibility, even likelihood, of

such recuperative readings, it is apparent that dramatic monologue, and the further range of play with personae, narrators and frameworks in Tennyson's writing, signal a shift in attitude to the role of the poet. I have suggested elsewhere that dramatic monologue enabled Victorian poets to evade the inconveniences of the Romantic 'I': the demand, generated in Romantic poetry, for complete visionary integrity in every first-person utterance limited the scope and flexibility of the lyric 'I'. Dramatic monologue, previously an occasional device, became invaluable because it readmitted the range of obliquity which pre-Romantic poets had been able to exploit.[47] I showed in chapter 2 how Shelley's confident vision depended upon the conjunction of political and imaginative liberty, and how the authority of this Romantic 'I' came to seem hardly sustainable to Tennyson. He was faced, instead, with the choices: relegation, incorporation, marginalization. These choices were unsatisfactory individually and bewildering together. Tithonus is often proposed as a figure of the poet: in the terms I have offered, he is the marginalized or relegated poet, 'at the quiet limit of the world', cut off from 'the kindly race of men', pleading: 'Release me, and restore me to the ground' (lines 7, 29, 72). I shall say more in the final chapter about the poet's relationship with an unprecedentedly immense public; here it will be sufficient to note *In Memoriam* (77) where gloom about the future of poetry is expressed:

> What hope is here for modern rhyme
>   To him, who turns a musing eye
>   On songs, and deeds, and lives, that lie
> Foreshortened in the tract of time?
>
> These mortal lullabies of pain
>   May bind a book, may line a box,
>   May serve to curl a maiden's locks.

The proliferation of personae and framing devices in Tennyson's poetry indicates lack of confidence in the poetic

'I', a feeling that if left to stand simply for itself it will be misunderstood or not carry conviction. 'The Palace of Art', 'Morte d'Arthur' and *The Princess* have prefaces or conclusions to elucidate their meanings and justify their methods. The preface to 'The Palace of Art' ('To — . With the Following Poem') is particularly ironic, for whilst the great part of that poem is indeed, as Tennyson says in the preface, 'a sort of allegory . . . of a soul . . . That did love Beauty only', that whole theme of the proper relations between beauty, goodness and knowledge in poetry is overshadowed by the fact that an introductory paragraph is necessary because the tale cannot be trusted to secure its message. Art may make its palaces and worry that it is being indulgent in so doing, but a much wider question is raised by the doubt whether it can make its point in the contemporary world.

Finally, we may be able to perceive the issue of fictive or feigning speakers as an alternative attempt to resolve the same problem that the symbolic mode, the attempted plenitude of the sign, was addressing. Foucault in *The Order of Things* invokes Mallarmé's attempt to fill up language – to enclose 'all possible discourse within the fragile density of the word, within that slim, material black line traced by ink upon paper'[48] – as a response to the kind of anxiety provoked by Nietzsche's assault upon subjectivity. Nietzsche referred questions of good and evil not to essences but to the speaker, destroying the certainties in relation to which subjectivity customarily positions itself. So, Foucault writes,

> To the Nietzschean question: 'Who is speaking?', Mallarmé replies – and constantly reverts to that reply – by saying that what is speaking is, in its solitude, in its fragile vibration, in its nothingness, the word itself – not the meaning of the word, but its enigmatic and precarious being. (*The Order of Things*, p. 305)

In such an extreme instance of the symbolic mode, the poet seeks to efface herself or himself altogether, to write as if the words have constituted themselves: thus they might achieve the reunification of language and the world. But the question 'Who is speaking?' is also that of dramatic monologue. At the simplest level, the monologue introduces a degree of ethical relativism, shows that opinions are specific to speakers; at the largest level, it disperses the claim of the author to power over his or her medium, inhibits identification of an originating consciousness, redistributes the poetic 'I' over a range of subjectivities. It is an alternative way of pursuing Mallarmé's project of effacing himself from his own language, of acknowledging the impossibility of the unified self and the motivated sign, in the hope of thereby retrieving some remnant of their vanished power. Such nostalgia is intrinsic to the characteristic Tennysonian melancholy – in Ulysses' wish 'To strive, to seek, to find, but not to yield', in Tithonus' plea 'Release me, and restore me to the ground', in the hope that Arthur will come again.

5 The Importance of Arthur Being

The Strategy of *In Memoriam*

The 3,000 lines written over seventeen years which make up *In Memoriam* witness to Tennyson's grief and anxiety at the death of Arthur Hallam. As I observed in chapter 3, the poem turns upon an experience, in section 95, very like Tennyson's trances, in which 'individuality itself seems to dissolve and fade away into boundless being' (*Memoir*, p. 168). Tennyson manages, almost, to install his dead friend in the space reserved for the Nameless, as the transcendental signified which would finally guarantee the fulness of all our mundane signs. Also, Tennyson's persistence with his elegies witnesses to his intuition that this theme and manner answer very well to the difficulties and objectives of the mid-nineteenth-century poet, as I have discussed them so far in this book: those of negotiating a role for poetry in a developing bourgeois hegemony, addressed typically by constructing poetry as a superior mode of language. Hence Tennyson's success, for most of his readers, in centring himself as the natural laureate of that culture. Nevertheless, such an ideal resolution cannot be complete and, indeed, it is likely to raise new complications.

We can see in the earliest written sections of *In Memoriam* how Tennyson struck immediately upon a vein which enabled him to write with a density of structure and resonance of personal and symbolic yearning. Section 30, written in 1833–4, has a structure almost as explicit as 'Now sleeps the crimson petal'. The opening two stanzas relate feeling to landscape: the Christmas eve of the family fell sadly as 'A rainy cloud possessed the earth' and they made only 'vain pretence/Of gladness'. The shape of the next four stanzas is set by 'We paused' and 'We ceased' at the start of the first and third; revising the poem between 1842 and 1845, Tennyson enhanced this effect by writing 'And silence followed' at the end of the third, corresponding to the silence at the end of the first (instead of 'We kissed each other').

> We paused: the winds were in the beech:
>   We heard them sweep the winter land;
>   And in a circle hand-in-hand
> Sat silent, looking each at each.
>
> Then echo-like our voices rang;
>   We sung, though every eye was dim,
>   A merry song we sang with him
> Last year: impetuously we sang:
>
> We ceased: a gentler feeling crept
>   Upon us: surely rest is meet:
>   'They rest', we said, 'their sleep is sweet',
> And silence followed, and we wept.
>
> Our voices took a higher range;
>   Once more we sang: 'They do not die
>   Nor lose their mortal sympathy,
> Nor change to us, although they change'.

Initially, in the first stanza quoted, the outside scene figures the family's discouragement and they hold hands in a circle against it, seeking containment and reciprocity within the human; the syntactic structure moves against the rhyme scheme, coherence is precarious. The song they sing in the second stanza is backward-looking, last year's, and again the stanza form is disturbed, suggesting their hesitancy and precipitate commitment. The silence of the third stanza is different from that of the first (repetition with difference is the primary strategy in the incremental structure of *In Memoriam*). The outside scene no longer impinges and the family feeling is no longer an echo or forced; the silence frees explicit grief and, in the fourth stanza, singing in 'a higher range', reaching beyond the mortal. The diction so far is relatively (perhaps surprisingly) conversational, but the syntax corresponds increasingly with the stanza shape and there is increasing use of incantatory repetition. These effects intensify as the last two stanzas give the rest of their song, and a concluding hymn of the poet which is both more personal and more general:

> 'Rapt from the fickle and the frail
>   With gathered power, yet the same,
>   Pierces the keen seraphic flame
> From orb to orb, from veil to veil'.

> Rise, happy morn, rise, holy morn,
>   Draw forth the cheerful day from night:
>   O Father, touch the east, and light
> The light that shone when Hope was born.

As Tennyson envisages a realm beyond the human, the writing becomes incantatory – poetic music seems to fill up the sign and remedy the defect of language – guaranteeing, as it seems, the metaphysical reality toward which it points. Thus it is the family's singing which gives them confidence in something which transcends mortality: in the silences they experience emotions beyond language, but the singing both represents and goes beyond those emotions.[1]

Arthur's soul is said to advance 'With gathered power, yet the same'. Here in an early poem we see already the characteristic incremental strategy of *In Memoriam*: the stanza form is repeated and within it phrases, images and syntactical structures are taken up and developed, and through it all there is an onward and upward movement which manages, still, to keep in touch with its starting point. This effect may be seen as giving to the whole sequence the harmony and unity which, from Tennyson's time to the present, has been taken as the hallmark of art's transcendence. The original reviewers mostly discovered such a unity:

The *Morning Post* said, 'Not only is the unity of design and of subject apparent throughout, but the thoughts follow each other in a natural sequence, the continuity of which renders it necessary to contemplate the work as a whole in order fully to appreciate its beauties'. The *Eclectic* declared, 'An organic unity informs the whole; unity of feeling and of interest'. And Lushington in *Tait's* asserted that the poem was 'perfect and unique as a whole, to a degree and in a style very rarely reached'.[2]

Section 30 – and this is the measure of Tennyson's immediate intuition of how these poems could work for him – anticipates not only the characteristic structural movement of *In Memoriam* but even its thematic development. The section moves from grief, concrete localities and personal circumstances to hope, an explicitly transcendent notion of reality and a more public discourse – the last stanza, especially, is like a hymn.[3] Reviewers appreciated this generalizing movement. The *Examiner* said it 'is a pathetic tale of real human sorrow . . . with varied and profound reflections on individual man, on society, and on their mutual relations'; and the *Eclectic* saw an 'outlet of personal feeling and sympathies' whose 'expression is enlarged into relevance with universal humanity'.[4]

The significance of *In Memoriam* was that it seemed to validate and even extend the current construction of poetry. I showed in chapter 2 that the main alternatives for poetry in the wake of the Shelleyan conjunction of political and imaginative freedom were the exploration of states of mind and direct incorporation into the hegemonic ideology. In *In Memoriam* Tennyson attempts to refuse the marginalization implicit in the cultivation of intense states of mind: he explores a personal grief, but asserts nevertheless that it is of universal significance. Thus he lays claim to a poetic 'I' that can stand without the indirection of dramatic monologue.

Now that we are familiar with the poem, it takes a little thought to recover the boldness of its strategy – even Tennyson did not at first see quite how much he could include. In 1842 he was planning a poem whose pretensions were not much larger than his personal elegy for Arthur Hallam.[5] The sections acknowledging the limited scope of his writing were in it (now 48, 49, 75, 76, 77) and there was little to contradict them.

> If these brief lays, of Sorrow born,
>   Were taken to be such as closed
>   Grave doubts and answers here proposed,
> Then these were such as men might scorn.
>
> (section 48)

But the poem as published in 1850 has much larger pretensions, and its readers by and large accepted them. It takes up troublesome issues like science, religion and political change and declares that 'all is well', claiming that its speculations are validated by the intensity of the poet's imaginative experience, by love:

> And if the song were full of care,
>   He breathed the spirit of the song;
>   And if the words were sweet and strong
> He set his royal signet there.
>
> (section 125)

In effect, as Terry Eagleton argues, Arthur 'is nothing less than the empty space congregated by a whole set of ideological anxieties concerned with science, religion, the class-struggle, in short with the "revolutionary" de-centring of "man" from his "imaginary" relation of unity with his world'.[6] (To avoid suppressing the intimacy of the poem, which some perhaps find embarrassing, I am writing 'Arthur' where commentators normally put 'Hallam'. In the text, after all, he is 'Arthur' and we wouldn't think of calling Beatrice or Laura by their formal second names.)

In the terms I used earlier, the margins bid for centrality. Tennyson repudiates the choice between individual states of mind and the major concerns of his society, and challenges directly the positivism of the ideology of machinery:

> I trust I have not wasted breath:
>   I think we are not wholly brain,
>   Magnetic mockeries.

> (section 120)

He denies that poetry is 'wasted breath', it has its own, superior validity, founded in the spiritual nature of humanity. Of course, all these assertions are insecure, shot through with 'doubt'. But that is not the point. The faith/doubt 'question' proclaims in its very construction the priority of 'spiritual' matters which poetry, in that culture, seemed specially equipped to handle, and the fact that 'faith' is always just beyond grasp suits excellently the strategies and themes of loss and yearning which Tennyson was perfecting.

Yet the transfigured Arthur affords only an apparent resolution. It is more interesting and necessary, now, to read *In Memoriam* for the discontinuities which convey a more complex sense of the human subject and its insertion in history and ideology. I pointed in chapter 3 towards Tennyson's awareness of the limitations of the self/ Nameless opposition: by projecting his love onto eternity he forgoes the human contact which was its motive force. Tennyson remarked to James Knowles about section 47: 'Love protests against the loss of identity in the theory of absorption'.[7] Yet absorption is pretty much what has happened to Arthur by the end. In section 82 the poet complains, 'We cannot hear each other speak' and in 130 he declares, 'Thy voice is on the rolling air.' But they are two different things, the connection is little more than metaphorical. Tennyson's discomfort with this shuffle is manifested quintessentially in section 95, where he wrote 'His living soul was flashed on mine,/And mine in his was wound', but changed it in 1872 to 'The living soul' and 'mine in this'. Tennyson commented: 'The Deity, maybe. The first reading . . . troubled me, as perhaps giving a wrong impression.' Neither 'impression' is adequate because, to close the argument of *In Memoriam*, Tennyson needs it to be *both* Arthur *and* the deity. The awkwardness of the attempt at closure has been argued recently by James R. Kincaid, Kerry McSweeney and Peter Hinchcliffe. Kincaid, somewhat hampered by the allegedly archetypal system of Northrop Frye, finds that *In Memoriam* does not move securely from the 'ironic' to the 'comic' pattern: from section 100 'the assurances lose power and images of profound irony intrude' and 'instead of a genuine conclusion, we are given a series of skilful but inadequate substitutes.'[8] McSweeney is keen to distinguish 'Romantic naturalism', which sees 'man as most creatively alive and most rooted when in vital reciprocal contact with the world around him', from supernaturalist religion, and he stresses the extent to which Tennyson tries to force the one to become the other.[9] Hinchcliffe doubts that Hallam can 'really be type and friend at the same time' and argues that although the concluding epithalamium may take 'the subsidiary anxieties of the sequence and close them off, one by one', it cannot 'finally divert us from the emptiness of heart with which *In Memoriam* ends. For Arthur Hallam has not been recovered and retained.'[10]

The split between the earthly and heavenly Arthurs appears precisely in Tennyson's ideas about how to preserve what I called, in chapter 2, bourgeois freedom. We are told that Arthur had

> A love of freedom rarely felt,
>   Of freedom in her regal seat
>   Of England; not the schoolboy heat,
> The blind hysterics of the Celt.

> (section 109)

His would have been

> A life in civic action warm,
> A soul on highest mission sent,
> A potent voice of Parliament,
> A pillar steadfast in the storm,
>
> Should licensed boldness gather force.
>
> (section 113)

The last line quoted and the ensuing seven were taken by Tennyson from 'Hail Briton!', the longest and most elaborate of the poems of 1831–3 about bourgeois freedom. From this we can see the specific role designed for Arthur: it is the role taken in the seventeenth-century English Revolution by John Hampden. In 'Hail Briton!' Hampden is invoked as 'A single voice before the strife . . . In whom the spirit of law prevailed/To war with edicts' (lines 59, 61–2); in 'England and America in 1782' bourgeois freedom is traced to 'that deep chord which Hampden smote'. Hampden's main role was as a parliamentarian, one who, as Tennyson imagines of Arthur, 'tracts of calm from tempest made' (112) – Macaulay admires him for his judicious pacification of the House of Commons: '"We had sheathed our swords in each other's bowels", says an eye-witness, "had not the sagacity and great calmness of Mr Hampden, by a short speech, prevented it'."[11]

Within the terms of nineteenth-century parliamentary politics, the role required of Arthur and the implicit programme for society are clear enough. But suppose they prove inadequate? The agrarian and Reform Bill disturbances of 1830–2 had been followed in England by Chartism, which had presented petitions for universal male suffrage to parliament in 1839, 1842 and 1848; in France, Germany, Italy, Hungary and Ireland there had been revolutionary uprisings in 1848. This is what Tennyson meant by 'licensed boldness gather[ing] force', 'the red fool-fury of the Seine' and 'The blind hysterics of the Celt' (113, 127, 109). His imagery in *In Memoriam* is that of earthquake and volcano –

> They tremble, the sustaining crags;
> The spires of ice are toppled down,
>
> And molten up, and roar in flood;
> The fortress crashes from on high,
> The brute earth lightens to the sky,
> And the great Æon sinks in blood.

(section 127)

The imagery was not uncommon. Joseph Stephens told a Poor Law repeal meeting in 1838: 'England stands on a mine – a volcano is beneath her; you may dance on it – you may pluck the flowers from its surface, but it only sleeps.'[12] It represented a recognition, perhaps obscure, that a discontented proletariat is not an occasional malfunction in the bourgeois state but a necessary contradiction at its deepest foundation.[13] Can Arthur's 'reverence and charity' cope with such a profound source of disturbance? – this was the class fear of 1848.

When Hampden had failed to control the situation through parliament, he took up arms and died fighting against the king's army (as Tennyson notes in 'Hail Briton!', 63–4). But Arthur is not envisaged as doing this. Of course, Hampden was fighting *for* the revolution, for bourgeois freedom against oppressive monarchy; Arthur is to defend the status quo against a new claim for freedom. Perhaps this is why, in the face of this ultimate threat, and with his uneasy negotiation of bourgeois freedom out of imaginative and political freedom, Tennyson has no political programme. Having failed to achieve bourgeois ends through parliament Arthur is withdrawn neatly to his fall-back position in eternity:

> thou, dear spirit, happy star,
> O'er lookst the tumult from afar,
> And smilest, knowing all is well.

(section 127)

The earthly Arthur is a model for a parliamentary statesman, but when the situation becomes more extreme the spiritual closure is called for – 'A deeper voice across the storm' rather than 'A potent voice of Parliament' (127, 113). The function of the heavenly Arthur – to handle that which cannot be coped with by human means – is apparent.

The Work as Polygraphy

Even as the idea that a work of art is a coherent structure leads back to the author as its coherent origin, so, contrariwise, an analysis of the significant failure of the structure of *In Memoriam* may lead us to consideration of the troubled subjectivity of the poet. Criticism has exercised itself to discover organic unity in the sequence. But Tennyson acknowledged that his way of writing was haphazard ('if there were a blank space I would put in a poem'); in 1842 he drew up two versions ending with section 57; he altered the arrangement and added sections up to and beyond the first printing; he said it didn't represent his views ('It's too hopeful, this poem, more than I am myself'); and in 1870–1 he was still thinking of extending it.[14] This history of course need not prevent us from looking for the structure which Tennyson (we might think) was chipping intuitively out of the block of his experience. But it may encourage us, alternatively, to see the poem as 'an uneasy mixture of a referential language and a rhetorically and psychically determined one', showing that 'there's no unified subject and no given plenitude for the poem to compose or enact.' These suggestions are Ann Wordsworth's.[15] I would not want to go along with her endorsement of Harold Bloom's reinstatement of literary history as an Oedipal psychodrama enacted, it would seem, on a desert island; but she is right to say that customary readings protect readers from 'the subversive and unorthodox aspects of the work' (p. 217).

The perplexities and incoherences of subjectivity are a recurrent concern in the poem. Initially the poet is disturbed at an abrupt alternation of 'calm despair and wild unrest' (16), but his more persistent anxiety is that the variety of his writing witnesses to an instability of commitment and identity. On each occasion he asserts an underlying continuity, but what is so revealing is that the terms of it change. At the second Christmas he asks:

> O sorrow, then can sorrow wane?
> O grief, can grief be changed to less?
>
> O last regret, regret can die!
>   No – mixt with all this mystic frame,
>   Her deep relations are the same,
> But with long use her tears are dry.

(section 78)

In section 125 the poet's continuity of feeling – in effect of identity – is asserted again, but now in terms of an allegedly consistent optimism:

> Yet Hope had never lost her youth;
>   She did but look through dimmer eyes;
>   Or Love but played with gracious lies,
> Because he felt so fixed in truth.

The alternatives here witness to the poet's difficulty: neither quite acounts for what he has written and together they undermine each other. Finally in the Epilogue he says that time has 'Remade the blood and changed the frame', and admits that he has changed:

> Regret is dead, but love is more
>   Than in the summers that are flown,
>   For I myself with these have grown
> To something greater than before.

(lines 17–20)

Yet another principle of consistency is offered here: change is made comprehensible through the idea of growth. But this entails a partial ('half') repudiation of the foregoing writing – it

> makes appear the songs I made
> As echoes out of weaker times,
> As half but idle brawling rhymes,
> The sport of random sun and shade.

                                                    (lines 21–4)

Tennyson's final theory of subjectivity rejects earlier theories of coherence and permanence: his writing is not the representation of a unified self.

An alternative way of thinking about *In Memoriam* may be drawn from *Roland Barthes by Roland Barthes*. This volume of autobiographical reminiscences and reflections, composed of brief sections, is like Tennyson's poem, but Barthes' aim is to prevent a structure from forming: 'Perhaps in places, certain fragments seem to follow one another by some affinity; but the important thing is that these little networks not be connected, that they not slide into a single enormous network which would be the structure of the book, its meaning'.[16] If that happened, it would appear that Barthes had represented a coherent self. He resists this because 'What I write about myself is never *the last word* . . . my texts are disjointed, no one of them caps any other; the latter is nothing but a *further* text, the last of the series, not the ultimate in meaning: *text upon text*, which never illuminates anything' (p. 120). One way by which Barthes maintains this indeterminacy is like Tennyson's use of dramatic monologue: he uses 'he' of himself to resist any easy resort to an 'I' figure by the reader.

Tennyson's inability to discover a unifying principle for his writing in individual subjectivity occurs because, at least in the case of *In Memoriam*, his relationship to his writing was much more like Barthes' than nineteenth-century assumptions about well-shaped poems enabled him to acknowledge. The sections do not, in Barthes' word, 'cap' each other; none of them, especially the last, is 'the last word'. There is no authentic shape to discover. Barthes says of himself: 'He more or less remembers the order in which he wrote these fragments; but where did that order come from? In the course of what classification, of what succession? He no longer remembers' (p. 148). We can see in the manuscripts something of Tennyson's processes of classification, and they witness to diverse purposes, conceived from time to time; that he too could not remember what his intention had been is shown by his divergent accounts of the poem; and in 1885 he allowed Palgrave to print in his *Lyrical Poems* a selection from *In Memoriam* with the sections in another order.

In the fourth edition (1851) Tennyson added section 59 (written earlier) at the point where he had once thought of ending the poem. In it he asserts once more the continuity and coherence of his identity but admits also the complex and indeterminate nature of his writing:

> My centred passion cannot move,
>   Nor will it lessen from today;
>   But I'll have leave at times to play
> As with the creature of my love;
>
> And set thee [i.e. Sorrow] forth, for thou art mine,
>   With so much hope for years to come,
>   That, howsoe'er I know thee, some
> Could hardly tell what name were thine.

Here Tennyson insists on the stability of his 'centred passion', but suggests that readers may hardly recognize the 'name' of his experience from his words. He does not, like the post-structuralist Barthes, acknowledge that the waywardness of writing points to the instability of the self, but he does detach his claim for stability from his writing, offering that writing as a space in which subjectivity moves rather than a representation of its coherence. I think of Tennyson during the composition of *In Memoriam* as rather like Barthes:

> I delight continuously, endlessly, in writing as in a perpetual production, in an unconditional dispersion, in an energy of seduction which no legal defense of the subject I fling upon the page can any longer halt.

> But in our mercantile society, one must end up with a
> work, an *'oeuvre'*: one must construct, i.e. *complete*, a
> piece of merchandise. (*Roland Barthes*, p. 136)

Tennyson was reluctant to publish his elegies (Ricks, *Poems*,
p. 856).

When the poem was published, Tennyson was still
worried that its poetic 'I' would be misconstrued. 'It must
be remembered that this is a poem, *not* an actual
biography', he insisted (Ricks, *Poems*, p. 859). The peculiar
nature of *In Memoriam* gives body to Paul de Man's general
proposition: 'It appears, then, that the distinction between
fiction and autobiography is not an either/or polarity but
that it is undecidable.'[17] In a sense all writing is autobiography, and the proclaimed instance of autobiography
'merely makes explicit the wider claim to authorship that
takes place whenever a text is stated to be *by* someone and
assumed to be understandable to the extent that this is the
case' (de Man, pp. 921–2). Tennyson's instance is the more
teasing because the title page of the first edition did *not* give
the author's name; but, in general, we do not separate the
intelligibility of a text from our sense that it is someone's
writing – Tennyson's initial readers quickly reinstated the
absent author.[18] The proclaimed autobiography demonstrates that, as all texts are autobiographies, so none of them
can be: there is no self-knowledge – no self – that can be
reliably inferred from writing.

De Man continues: 'The name on the title page is not the
proper name of a subject capable of self-knowledge and
understanding, but the signature that gives the contract
legal, though by no means epistemological, authority'
('Autobiography as de-facement', p. 922). The inseparabil-
ity of autobiography and fiction demonstrates the instability of the text in its successive moments of composition and
in its relations with readers: it is our choice how far, or in
what sense, we accept the contract proposed on the title
page. The signature may be 'Tennyson', but meaning is
always negotiated in reception, in particular discourses and

historical conditions. Successive attempts – in each critical book and essay – to ascribe a secure meaning to the text and its named author are appropriations of their authority, rather than identifications of a coherent originating consciousness. And Tennyson, despite acceding to the demand for a completed work, an *oeuvre*, has left us the opportunity to read 'the work as polygraphy' (*Roland Barthes*, p. 148).

Feminine and Masculine

The other great challenge offered by *In Memoriam* is its treatment of same-sex love.

> Tears of the widower, when he sees
>   A late-lost form that sleep reveals,
>   And moves his doubtful arms, and feels
> Her place is empty, fall like these;
>
> Which weep a loss for ever new,
>   A void where heart on heart reposed;
>   And, where warm hands have prest and closed,
> Silence, till I be silent too.

(section 13)

The most striking thing about this analogy is certainly its inappropriateness. When Queen Victoria 'substituted "widow" for "widower" and "her" for "his"' in these lines[19] she did more than switch genders, she adapted the poem to a relationship in which a shared bed legitimately featured.

The whole closure which the poem seeks to enact depends upon 'love' and the transfigured Arthur and this, as everyone from Tennyson onwards remarks, is reminiscent of Dante's *Divine Comedy*. What is almost never acknowledged is that Dante's great contribution to western culture was an authoritative translation of the ideal construction of homosexual love, as it was received from the Greeks, into a more amenable heterosexual form, and that *In Memoriam* threatens to reverse this convenient move. The other analogues are if anything more disturbing. One, as Shatto and Shaw have recently pointed out (*In Memoriam*, pp. 26–9), is the Latin love elegy sequence, and this poetry took as theme both heterosexual and homosexual attraction, and treated it, very often, in explicit sexual language. The other analogue is the other major love poetry in English written by a man about a man, Shakespeare's sonnets. Of the sonnets Arthur Hallam's father complained in 1869: 'it is impossible not to wish that Shakespeare had never written them. There is a weakness and folly in all excessive and mis-placed affection, which is not redeemed by the touches of nobler sentiments' (Ricks, *Poems*, p. 861). Arthur Hallam's own contributions to the heterosexualizing of the European love tradition point up the boldness of Tennyson's move. They include a poem of 700 lines ('A Farewell to the South') in which Beatrice is proposed as a model for nineteenth-century women; a brisk assimilation of Shakespeare's sonnets to the same 'mode of sentiment' by taking them at the extremely abstract level of 'a sort of homage to that Genius of Christian Europe' (i.e. Dantesque love); and a bland regret at the 'misunderstanding' of 'that frequent commendation of a more lively sentiment than has existed in other times between man and man . . . which has repelled several from the deep tenderness and splendid imaginations of the Phaedrus and the Symposium'.[20]

The cleaning up of *In Memoriam* was promoted by Tennyson's son, who deleted from Benjamin Jowett's letter the sentences: 'It would not have been manly or natural to have lived in it always' – i.e. in 'the great sorrow of his own mind', and 'The love of the sonnets [Shakespeare's] which he so strikingly expressed was a sort of sympathy with Hellenism' (Ricks, *Poems*, p. 860). The general failure of twentieth-century criticism to discuss the issue is a scandal. Stephen Greenblatt has observed, shrewdly, 'we locate as "subversive" in the past precisely those things that are *not* subversive to ourselves, that pose no threat to the order by which we live and allocate resources.'[21] In the case of *In Memoriam*, criticism has made much of science and religious doubt, which are no longer issues for most educated people, but a subversion of mainstream constructions of sexuality is either explained away or, even more firmly, not discussed at all.

In the 1970s the Gay Liberation movement made it more difficult to ignore the issue. Robert Martin in his biography nevertheless takes it rather rapidly, concluding that Tennyson 'was not a deeply sexual man, and that his emotional needs at Cambridge were largely fulfilled by his friendship with Hallam, probably making the love of a woman less necessary for him than it would otherwise have been'.[22] Christopher Ricks in his *Tennyson* is characteristically probing. He brings up most of the awkward evidence – Jowett's suppressed comment and Henry Hallam's nervousness; 'some particular turns of speech which disconcert', such as the words deleted from 93: 'Stoop soul and touch me: wed me' – and, indeed, the published version, 'Descend, and touch, and enter', which, Ricks remarks, 'is in some ways even more disconcerting'; the complaints and misapprehensions of some reviewers; and a strange letter from Tennyson, replying to James Spedding's humorous suggestion that Hallam 'slept with' him, assuring Spedding that 'we have a spare bed.'[23] Ricks concludes, somewhat obscurely, that a certain 'privacy limits the nature of *In Memoriam* – but it also provides some of its sources of energy' (p. 221).

The issue can be discussed productively only in the light of nineteenth-century constructions of sexuality and gender. As Jeffrey Weeks explains, it is a mistake to conceptualize sex as a dehistoricized 'driving, instinctual force, whose characteristics are built into the biology of the human animal, which shapes human institutions and whose will must force its way out, either in the form of direct sexual expression or, if blocked, in the form of perversion or neuroses'.[24] The view which corresponds to the materialist emphasis taken in the present study, and which is offered by Lacan, Foucault and interactionist social scientists like J. H. Gagnon and William Simon, sees 'the individual as a product of social forces, an "ensemble of social relations", rather than as a simple natural unity' (Weeks, p. 3). In this view sexuality is not a given which must find its way to the surface by one means or another, it is, rather, something which is constructed in determinate historical conditions. The basic point was made by John Stuart Mill in *The Subjection of Women* (1869), when he denied that the current arrangements between men and women were 'natural', pointing out that every oppressive relation (slavery, absolute monarchy, feudalism) is imagined by its perpetrators to be natural:

> I deny that anyone knows, or can know, the nature of the two sexes, as long as they have only been seen in their present relation to one another. If men had ever been found in society without women, or women without men, or if there had been a society of men and women in which the women were not under the control of the men, something might have been positively known about the mental and moral differences which may be inherent in the nature of each. What is now called the nature of women is an eminently artifical thing – the result of forced repression in some directions, unnatural stimulation in others.[25]

Mill still allows that there may be some essential qualities beneath particular social arrangements, but the conclusion that 'it all depends' is there to be drawn.

The Victorians did not, as we are liable to imagine, repress sexuality; on the contrary, they thought and wrote and talked about it a great deal and turned it into the discourse to which all else can be referred. 'Homosexuality' was invented (the word was not coined until 1869 and did not enter English currency until the 1890s)[26] as part of what Foucault has analysed as an intensification and enlargement of the production of sexuality in discourse: 'legal sanctions against minor perversions were multiplied; sexual irregularity was annexed to mental illness; from childhood to old age, a norm of sexual development was defined and all the possible deviations were carefully described; pedagogical controls and medical treatments were organized; around the least fantasies, moralists, but especially doctors, brandished the whole emphatic vocabulary of abomination.'[27] The process is like that which we saw in chapter 2, whereby modes of experience not directly compatible with the developing bourgeois hegemony were pushed into marginal positions. From there, not only could they hardly threaten the dominant ideology, also, through their marginality, they affirmed its centrality.

Weeks identifies four kinds of nineteenth-century 'homosexual' (as we would call it) experience: 'the casual encounter, which rarely touches the self-concept'; 'the highly individualized, the deeply emotional, sometimes even sexual, relation between two individuals who are otherwise not regarded, or do not regard themselves, as "deviant"' (this would be Tennyson's case); the 'situational: activity which may be regarded as legitimate in certain circumstances, for example in schools or the army and navy or prisons'; and fourth, 'a total way of life . . . involvement in an identity and sub-culture which, with its own system of values and ideologies, is the obvious forerunner of that of the present day.'[28] The 'discursive explosion' (Foucault's term) of the nineteenth century tended to drive male homosexual experience into the fourth category, facilitating both persecution and eventually, after many people had suffered bitterly, the formation of a homosexual identity strong enough in itself to resist that persecution.

There is no reason to assume that Tennyson's 'deeply emotional' attachment to Arthur Hallam was 'really' a suppressed or repressed instance of the fourth category: there is no essential form behind the particular social construction. At the same time, the fact that the relationship perhaps was not directly sexual, or perhaps was just momentarily so (at Cauteretz?), does not mean that we can heave a sigh of relief and relax because they were just good friends. Such intensity of male bonding was situated ambiguously and provocatively in the complex field of nineteenth-century sexuality. As in our own time, sex and gender were sites of struggle across which people contested opposing patterns of behaviour, within a context of changing class and power relations. The emotions represented in *In Memoriam* should be understood as in uneasy relation to the dominant notions of proper manly behaviour.

The developing bourgeois hegemony was aggressive, but it was also anxious and insecure – about the speed of industrialization and urbanization and the growth of a disaffected working class; and, largely from within the bourgeoisie itself, about the authority of traditional religion and the rights of women. Insistence on a rigid ideology of male and female characteristics and behaviour aspired to get at least one part of the system within control: in the family, Robert Gray suggests, 'ideologists of subordination and control (over women, children and servants) could be acted out, as they could not in the world of industrial production.'[29] Also, insistence on respectable domesticity asserted bourgeois superiority over both an effete and disreputable aristocracy and an allegedly lax and dirty working class. (Well before the end of the century those other classes had, in large part, adopted 'bourgeois standards'.)

Basically, females were supposed to be innocent until they were married, when they became wifely and maternal, though there were also 'fallen' women; men were subject to sexual temptation (hence the fallen women) but tried to channel it virtuously into marriage. Peter Cominos has remarked how this ideology corresponded with that of manufacture: homo economicus experiences conflicting motives – a productive desire for wealth opposes an aversion for labour and a debilitating desire for costly indulgences – and has to resolve this virtuously through 'good' qualities in his character. So it is with homo sensualis: his conflict is between a proper outlet for his sexuality and temptations to dissipation. The model for femina sensualis distributes the same items differently: this was 'a dual model, either innocent or tainted, in whom the conflict took place unconsciously for the innocent or consciously for the tainted, but not very intensely'.[30] So woman was constituted as both the object and the ratification of male desire.

The outcome is the image which seems to dispel the despondency of Tennyson's 'Two Voices':

> One walked between his wife and child,
> With measured footfall firm and mild,
> And now and then he gravely smiled.
>
> The prudent partner of his blood
> Leaned on him, faithful, gentle, good,
> Wearing the rose of womanhood.
>
> And in their double love secure,
> The little maiden walked demure,
> Pacing with downward eyelids pure.

(lines 412–20)

The limitation of the wife and maiden to roles which the man could dominate are the most evident effects here, but the image of the man repays attention. Between wife and child he controls both, but he is also held himself and his 'measured footfall' suggests determined self control. And what of the *grave* smiling, now and then? – when, and at what? I sense what Leonore Davidoff has called a 'psychological backlash' deriving from

> the effort of adult middle-class men to maintain their positions of power within the society as a whole and the 'little kingdoms' of their own households, as well as in regard to their own sexuality. . . . They combined excessive fears of pollution, disloyalty, and disorder from subordinates with a desperate search for a moral order which would help to control all three, as well as the immoral forces of the market.[31]

The function of ideology is to render coherent a social formation which is actually riven with conflict and contradiction. Tennyson's explorations of unconventional aspects of masculinity were conducted within a troubled and anxious ideological field.

The uncertainty of Tennyson's personal engagement with the prescribed images of the feminine is apparent in the unconvincing poems he published in 1830 and 1832 about perhaps imaginary young ladies. Equally, those written about Rosa Baring, for whom his 'love' in 1834–6 is said to have been 'one of the most important episodes of his life'[32] seem remarkably conventional:

> Thy rosy lips are soft and sweet,
> Thy fairy form is so complete,
> Thy motions are so airy free,
> Love lays his armour at thy feet
> And yields his bow to thee;
> Take any dart from out his quiver
> And pierce what heart thou wilt for ever.

Nonetheless, his published poems about young ladies were widely approved – by Hallam, Fox, Wilson and Mill; they were what people (?men) wanted to believe about maidens.[33] The wifely ideal seems to have had a more specific purchase for Tennyson, deriving from his admiration for the way his mother coped with the depression and alcoholism of his father. 'Isabel' evokes 'The stately flower of female fortitude,/Of perfect wifehood and pure lowlihead' but is rendered distinctive by the special demands made upon her by her 'wayward' husband:

> A clear stream flowing with a muddy one,
>   Till in its onward current it absorbs
>   With swifter movement and in purer light
>   The vexed eddies of its wayward brother:
>   A leaning and upbearing parasite,
>   Clothing the stem, which else had fallen quite.

The husband is the main stem and the wife the parasite,

but she keeps him upright; it is a vivid adaptation of traditional imagery.

The reasons for disturbing either the hierarchy or the rigid division between feminine and masculine were not just personal insecurity. Such disturbance was also a way of protecting against or disrupting the crude spirit of masculinist aggression which dominated commerce and industry. John Killham argues that 'the sympathetic, even chivalrous, attitude towards women is part of a strategy a main object of which is to attack the commercial ethos and to replace it by one having human welfare as its goal.'[34] Carol Christ has discussed a pattern in Victorian writers, and especially Coventry Patmore and Tennyson, of 'feminine identification and idealization' as a way of 'responding to a world in which action has lost its religious imperative and seems to have gained meaning only from a Malthusian and Darwinian marketplace'.[35] In the 1832 version of 'A Dream of Fair Women' Tennyson wrote:

> In every land I thought that, more or less,
>   The stronger sterner nature overbore
> The softer, uncontrolled by gentleness
>   And selfish evermore.

A more humane concept of society was expressed either by insisting on the virtues of women or by suggesting a fusion of supposed masculine and feminine qualities.

Terry Eagleton is severe on such a strategy in his essay 'Tennyson: politics and sexuality in *The Princess* and *In Memoriam*': he declares that in the Victorian period a 'brutally explicit *dominance* fails to secure the conditions of ruling-class *hegemony*' and therefore that hegemony seeks acceptability by deferring, in certain respects, to 'those "civilizing" values of "sweetness" and "moral nobility" which are paradigmatically "feminine"' (p. 97). In the larger perspective this is right: a system which seems to accommodate 'human values' will perhaps survive better in the conditions of modern capitalism. But at the same time we may note four principles which are liable to complicate both hegemony and any challenge to it in a complex society.[36] First, any subversive movement is likely to find itself working substantially within the terms set up by the dominant ideology – there is no place outside ideology from which a completely untainted critique can be mounted. Second and consequently, it is not uncommon for a movement which is progressive in one way to be oppressive in another (so, in this instance, a distrust of the dominant relations of capitalism is expressed through a disturbance of the terms 'masculine' and 'feminine' which, in order to achieve that disturbance, in effect affirms the validity of the sexist distinction). Third, short of proletarian revolution, positive developments are quite likely to come piecemeal through a dissident fraction of the middle class – within Victorian culture there was a continual exploitation of diverse opportunities for specific classes, fractions and categories to confirm or extend economic, political or ideological power, and although hegemony might incorporate dissident movements it could not do so entirely on its own terms. So even though dissident movements can be seen as helping to sustain the relations of production, their effect is not negligible. And fourth, how far a particular intervention represents a shrewd subversion and how far it leaves the dominant the stronger for being able to accommodate a critique, will rarely be within the control of a writer, for meaning is always negotiated in the conditions of reception. Overall, I see the confusion of gender categories as more difficult, then and now, for bourgeois hegemony to handle than Eagleton does. Although Tennyson may try eventually to close down the challenge, he is playing a risky game, one which is likely to leave uncomfortable residues.

The extent of the anxiety caused by 'effeminacy' may be gauged from the twists and turns undertaken by one strand of the movement to ameliorate the harshness of the dominant masculinist ideology. Charles Kingsley and Thomas Hughes tried to divert the cult of manliness which was growing in public schools, sport and male clubs into

'Christian manliness', hoping thus to combine individual moral and political potential with confidence in personal and social salvation through strenuous service.[37] They insisted on the manliness as well as the religion, and were keen to avoid appearing feminine. C. H. Spurgeon proclaimed: 'When I say that a man in Christ *is* a man, I mean that, if he be truly in Christ, he is therefore manly. There has got abroad a notion, somehow, that if you become a Christian you must sink your manliness and turn milksop.'[38] The difficulties are amusingly apparent in Hughes' *Tom Brown's Schooldays* (1857). Tom proves his manliness by uncooperative behaviour in the school, but Hughes wishes this to be tempered and introduces a 'new ' boy, Arthur, for whom Tom is made responsible. He seems an unmanly youngster – the kind who is 'always getting laughed at, and called Molly, or Jenny, or some derogatory feminine nickname'[39] – but when he kneels by his bed to pray Tom experiences a moral crisis (though after Dr Arnold's 'manly piety had begun to leaven the school' kneeling and praying became common, p. 200). So Tom kneels too and the other boys begin to follow his example and the sniggers stop – though 'this was in some measure owing to the fact, that Tom could probably have thrashed any boy in the room except the præpostor' (p. 202). So the effeminate Arthur has a salutary influence, but it is contained within the fundamental manliness of Tom – into which Arthur is in due course incorporated. What Hughes could not incorporate was 'the miserable little pretty white-handed curly-headed boys, petted and pampered by some of the big fellows'; for summoning Tom and East to 'fag' for a senior boy such a boy is shaken up, tripped so that he falls to the floor, jerked upright, threatened with a thrashing and sent 'flying into the quadrangle, with a parting kick' (pp. 206–7). More manly than Christian, perhaps. It may sound straightforward to propose that men should be more feminine, but unless carefully handled it could catch a raw nerve in Victorian ideology.

The scope and daring of Tennyson's involvement in

feminization was far more than personal. His topics and manner were what that society saw as women's stuff – the finer feelings and verbal arts, not the masculine concerns of utilitarianism, political economy and machinery. This was in part the role allocated to poetry within the developing bourgeois hegemony: even as poetry was pushed to the margins, so it was associated with the (allegedly) feminine. Both constructions acknowledged a certain alternative impetus in poetry and both were designed to contain that impetus. So Kingsley in *Two Years Ago* (1857) portrayed the effeminate poet Elsey Vavasour, author of *The Soul's Agonies*, as an unhealthy mind in an unhealthy body.[40] Bagehot's final thought on Tennyson's 'ornate' style is that it is the result of the influence of women, 'whose voice on literature counts as well as that of men – and . . . women, such as we know them, such as they are likely to be, ever prefer a delicate unreality to a true or firm art.'[41] And Aubrey de Vere remarked to a friend that there was but one person in London for whom he, de Vere, would keep late hours: 'a lady? Certainly, if as old Coleridge said, every true Poet is inclusively woman, but not the worse man on that account – Alfred Tennyson' (Martin, *Tennyson*, p. 288).

Tennyson made little effort, at least up till the publication of *In Memoriam*, to protect his writing from imputations of effeminacy. His delicacy of expression, cultivation of exquisite sensations and evocations of supposed feminine experience amounted to an alternative programme for his brutally efficient society. Even Fox was somewhat defensive: 'A considerable number of the poems are amatory; they are the expression not of heartless sensuality, nor of a sickly refinement, nor of fantastic devotion, but of manly love' (Armstrong, p. 80). Others were less sympathetic. Edward Bulwer in 1833 repeatedly accused Tennyson of the 'effeminacies' of the Cockney school and of 'a want of manliness in love . . . an eunuch strain'.[42] He referred especially to 'O Darling Room' (1832) which concluded:

A little room so exquisite,
With two such couches, soft and white;

> Not any room so warm and bright,
> Wherein to read, wherein to write.

John Croker also mocked this with sexual innuendo: 'In such a dear *little* room a narrow-minded scribbler would have been content with *one* sofa, and that one he would probably have covered with black mohair, or red cloth, or a good striped chintz; how infinitely more characteristic is white dimity! – 'tis as it were a type of the purity of the poet's mind.'[43] Robert Martin suggests that somewhere in Tennyson's mind was the room he had shared with Hallam at Somersby and wonders, had he said 'more than he intended, or even knew, about the nature of his affection for Hallam, and had Croker noticed this when Tennyson had not?' (*Tennyson*, pp. 171–2). The idea that Tennyson's poetry was effeminate stuck. In 1860 George Gilfillan spoke for the Spasmodic school of poetry when he criticized Tennyson because 'his fancy loves, better than is manly or beseeming, the tricksy elegancies of artificial life – the "white sofas" of his study – the trim walks of his garden – the luxuries of female dress – and all the tiny comforts and beauties which nestle round an English parlour.'[44] Carlyle thought Tennyson 'a life-guardsman spoilt by poetry'.[45]

That *The Princess* is a serious and complex engagement with contemporary feminist debates, allowing scope for a range of interpretation, is shown in John Killham's valuable study, *Tennyson and 'The Princess'* (London: Athlone, 1958). However, at the end of the poem Tennyson makes the women's educational community founder all too easily, through its inherent instability and the rival attractions of love and marriage. Ida is won to the role of wife and mother – it was there, underneath, all the time:

> all
> Her falser self slipt from her like a robe,
> And left her woman.
>
> (VII, 145–7)

What is less conservative is the presentation of the prince.

Hallam Tennyson says 'His too emotional temperament was intended from an artistic point of view to emphasize his comparative want of power' (p. 209). He is subject to the 'weird seizures' (discussed in chapter 3) and this is how he first appears:

> A prince I was, blue-eyed, and fair in face,
> Of temper amorous, as the first of May,
> With lengths of yellow ringlet, like a girl,
> For on my cradle shone the Northern star.
>
> (I, 1–4)

He does not endorse the extreme position of his unsubtle and aggressive father ('Man is the hunter; woman is his game' – V, 147) – this is the unacceptable bullying by established authority which Tennyson probably associated with his grandfather. The prince dresses in woman's clothes to pursue Ida, and when it comes to a battle he falls and goes into a trance. His wooing is tearful, 'all for languor and self-pity' (VII, 124), and it is the appeal to Ida's womanly piety which brings her around. As Carol Christ points out, the idealization of femininity makes it difficult to bring the man in such a narrative to the point where he can take positive action;[46] so the prince wins Ida through her predisposition to be won, and thus gender categories are reinstated – though without an endorsement of male aggression.

The terms which the prince proposes for the marriage envisage a convergence of (supposed) male and female attributes:

> Yet in the long years liker must they grow;
> The man be more of woman, she of man;
> He gain in sweetness and in moral height,
> Nor lose the wrestling thews that throw the world;
> She mental breadth, nor fail in childward care,
> Nor lose the childlike in the larger mind;
> Till at the last she set herself to man,
> Like perfect music unto noble words.
>
> (VII, 263–70)

As I have argued, we may view such a statement as partly progressive in its time. Nevertheless, it certainly reinstates the gender distinctions it purports to criticize – the last two lines ensure that. We may remark, with Mill, than 'men do not want solely the obedience of women, they want their sentiments. . . . They have therefore put everything in practice to enslave their minds.'[47]

Even so, with this move toward androgyny, Tennyson feels obliged to undertake some tricky manoeuvring in his attempt to make a positive conclusion for the prince credible. Ida asks him where he learnt his ideal of marriage – 'what woman taught you this?' –

> 'Alone', I said, 'from earlier than I know,
> Immersed in rich foreshadowings of the world,
> I loved the woman; he, that doth not, lives
> A drowning life, besotted in sweet self,
> Or pines in sad experience worse than death,
> Or keeps his winged affections clipt with crime'.
>
> (VII, 291–7)

Tennyson and the prince seem to know of alternatives to loving a woman – narcissism, loneliness, homosexuality ('clipt' means 'embraced'). Not only may masculine and feminine converge and overlap, therefore, there are other possibilities too, once we forsake the king's simple binary model. Some cancelled lines even propose to accommodate them:

> And if aught be comprising in itself
> The man, the woman, let it sit [apart]
> Godlike, alone, or only rapt on heaven –
> What need for such to wed? or if there be
> Men-women, let them wed with women-men
> And make a proper marriage.
>
> (Ricks, *Poems*, p. 838)

Examined closely, this perhaps doesn't say much, but its manner makes it sound as though quite unconventional relationships are envisaged.

The prince's explanation of what has enabled him to become heterosexual is, for us at least, problematic and revealing: it is the infant relationship with his mother, who is described in terms like those used in 'Isabel' (VII, 298–312). It is here that the poem makes a dash for safe closure, appealing to the maternal stereotype, but for post-Freudians, as Eagleton observes, the prince 'remains locked to the end in his Oedipal problems'.[48] Ida's response seems at first sight to say as much:

'It seems you love to cheat yourself with words:
This mother is your model. I have heard
Of your strange doubts: they well might be: I seem
A mockery to my own self. Never, Prince;
You cannot love me'.

(VII, 314–18)

But Tennyson does not intend us to construe Ida as saying that the prince is fixated on his mother: the prince takes her to mean that she cannot measure up to such a perfect example of womanhood and reassures her that she is indeed worthy of his love (318–29). This seems to be regarded in the poem as satisfactory; for Ida (like Isabella at the end of *Measure for Measure*) does not speak again to dispute it. The attachment to mother, it is suggested, is not a problem but the answer. The story ends twenty-two lines later, though perhaps with a residual anxiety, for the penultimate line suggests that manhood is not something of which the prince is possessed, but what he will receive through Ida's assumption of womanhood:

'Yield thyself up: my hopes and thine are one:
Accomplish thou my manhood and thyself;
Lay thy sweet hands in mine and trust to me'.

(VII, 343–5)

The maternal stereotype is offered as the completion of maleness and of the poem. Such an outcome was both necessary and necessarily unsatisfactory if Tennyson was finally to limit his critique of the 'masculine' to a negotiation within rather than a repudiation of the dominant ideology.

'I never even called him "dear"'

If *The Princess*, however insecurely, closes down the provocative idea of male femininity, *In Memoriam* certainly opens it up again. One initial reviewer who did not know of the poem's authorship declared, 'these touching lines evidently come from the full heart of the widow of a military man' (*Memoir*, p. 250). And why not? – our better knowledge is a good instance of the inevitable interference discussed in the opening pages of this book between author and text. *The Times*' reviewer complained:

> A second defect which has painfully come out as often as we take up the volume is the tone of – may we say so? – amatory tenderness. . . . Shakespeare may be considered the founder of this style in English. In classical and Oriental poetry it is unpleasantly familiar. We object to a Cantab being styled a 'rose' under any conditions. . . . We can appreciate the meditative rapture of Burns, who saw his 'Jean' in the flower under the hedge; but the taste is displeased when every expression of fondness is sighed out, and the only figure within our view is Amaryllis of the Chancery Bar.

Quoting section 74, he commented: 'Very sweet and plaintive these verses are, but who would not give them a feminine application?'[49]

T. S. Eliot said *In Memoriam* is 'the concentrated diary of a man confessing himself'.[50] Foucault has elaborated the role of confession as 'one of the West's most highly valued techniques for producing truth': 'It is no longer a question simply of saying what was done – the sexual act – and how it was done; but of reconstructing, in and around the act, the thoughts that recapitulated it, the obsessions that accompanied it, the images, desires, modulations, and quality of the pleasure that animated it.'[51] *In Memoriam* is not a reconstruction of a sexual act, as that is usually understood, but of a relationship notable for every deep and intimate form of interaction, it seems, but that. Foucault's point is that confessional writing does not reveal the truth of our most secret nature, which 'demands' only to surface; rather, confession positions human subjects so that they internalize dominant conceptions of subjectivity. *In Memoriam* seems to have served the function for Tennyson of *My Secret Life* and the sexual diaries of J. A. Symonds and A. J. Munby, each of whom was 'using the diary to construct a meaningful identity by using themes from his culture – both those that were explicitly admired and those that were forbidden – and reinterpreting them to fit his own psychic structure'.[52] So Tennyson produces Arthur and himself through modes of love writing which have been used before. None of them is 'forbidden', but often their deployment in this context activates awkward side effects or affords a noticeably inadequate fit. Tennyson was able to publish his writing, though only after a lot of hesitation and reworking.

> Dark house, by which once more I stand
>   Here in the long unlovely street,
>   Doors, where my heart was used to beat
> So quickly, waiting for a hand,
>
> A hand that can be clasped no more –
>   Behold me, for I cannot sleep,
>   And like a guilty thing I creep
> At earliest morning to the door.
>
>   (section 7)

This is one of the most intense sections of the poem, and it is also one of the more direct allusions to the classical love elegy. Shatto and Shaw identify it as from the minor genre 'in which the poet-lover stands outside the house of his mistress at night and laments that the door is bolted against him' (*In Memoriam*, p. 27; also p. 169). True, but the source of the theme and its most distinctive expression is the twenty-third idyll attributed to Theocritus, and this begins: 'A lover once pined for a heartless youth.'[53] This directly homosexual analogue is not the only influence upon our reading of section 7; there are heterosexual models, for instance by Tibullus and Propertius. But these produce Arthur as the poet's mistress, an equally awkward implication. The classical love elegy offered itself as a discourse for Tennyson to use, but the complexities set up through its derivation from cultures where sexuality was regarded very differently, together with the interaction of that with the unorthodoxy of Tennyson's feelings for Arthur, result in a disturbance of customary gender categories. It is not that Tennyson is revealed to have 'homosexual tendencies' – that would enable us to pigeon-hole him – but that there is no proper fit to be achieved with received discourses. (That Tennyson had this Theocritan poem in mind is clear in the partner section 119. Theocritus' lover complains: 'no flicker of the lip,/no twinkle in his eye'; Tennyson proclaims in similar terms the continuing presence of the absent loved one: 'thy lips are bland/And bright the friendship of thine eye'.)

Section 8 seems designed to bring some of the gender confusion of section 7 into better control by giving the poet, at least, a clear analogue – to a man in love with a woman:

A happy lover who has come
    To look on her that loves him well,
    Who 'lights and rings the gateway bell,
And learns her gone and far from home;

He saddens, all the magic light
    Dies off at once from bower and hall,
    And all the place is dark, and all
The chambers emptied of delight:

So find I every pleasant spot
    In which we two were wont to meet,
    The field, the chamber and the street,
For all is dark where thou art not.

It seems at first that the analogue is going to regularize the poet's feeling by lightening the mood – 'the magic light' is almost trivial, a young man's charming devotion, and the disappointment is probably temporary. The unorthodoxy of the poet's relationship doesn't matter so much if it is at a lower pressure. But the analogy cannot hold because his loss is permanent and the lighter mood collapses in the last line quoted: 'For all is dark where thou art not'. His feeling is not contained by the analogue, it appears the more intense and real, beyond customary experience.

Such domestic analogues constitute another approved discourse through which Tennyson tries to filter Arthur and himself. He tries the whole gamut of family relationships – he is father, mother and maiden lover (6), servants and children (20), father and mother of a bride (40), a deserted maiden (60, 62), a wife (97). Each comparison is problematic in itself, and the shifting from one to another highlights the difficulty. Always there is the danger of an unattributable excess of sexual implication. For section 97 Tennyson wrote a stanza expressing the physical intensity of a marriage, but he never published it:

> They madly drank each other's breath
>   With breast to breast in early years.
>   They met with passion and with tears,
> Their every parting was a death.

A third main language in which the Arthur–Tennyson relationship is produced is that of death and heaven. This may seem obvious, but what emerges has intimate implications which are easily transferred to an intense living relationship. Death makes Arthur not just absent but, as the poem has it, superior; the poet is not just bereaved, he is inferior. The explicit reason is that Arthur is a soul in heaven, but much more is implied. Perhaps he hardly even thinks of the poet, but is

> as one that once declined,
>   When he was little more than boy,

On some unworthy heart with joy,
  But lives to wed an equal mind;

And breathes a novel world, the while
  His other passion wholly dies,
  Or in the light of deeper eyes
Is matter for a flying smile.

(section 62)

Such writing is disturbing, embarrassing perhaps, because of the intimacy and intensity which it allows us to glimpse, the hints of how much Arthur meant to the poet and of a disparity in their feelings. Freud suggests that in a man of melancholic disposition there will be something more than is normally present in mourning: 'an extraordinary diminution in his self-regard, an improverishment of his ego on a grand scale. In mourning it is the world which has become poor and empty; in melancholia it is the ego itself.'[54] Moreover, in Freud's view, we should not take self-deprecation (like Tennyson's) at face value: 'we perceive that the self-reproaches are reproaches against a loved object which have been shifted away from it on to the patient's own ego' (p. 257). Resentment of Arthur is apparent in most of the poet's self-deprecation: usually there is an underlying implication that Arthur cannot be bothered with his old friend. Section 97 offers the analogue of a husband and wife who are no longer close because he is a great scientist. The situation is not entirely clear:

  Their love has never past away;
    The days she never can forget
    Are earnest that he loves her yet,
  Whate'er the faithless people say.

The assertion of the first line, that they both still love, is not supported; his love is in doubt. We are told, cryptically, 'He looks so cold: she thinks him kind.' The next stanza says he loves her, but it seems to be written as her perception, her wish-fulfilment, and in violation of the evidence:

Her life is lone, he sits apart,
   He loves her yet, she will not weep,
   Though rapt in matters dark and deep
He seems to slight her simple heart.

The problem is not just the demands of science; by any usual criteria the man is *unkind* and the poem exposes him. It concludes: 'She dwells on him with faithful eyes,/"I cannot understand: I love"'. It is not just the man's studies which are beyond comprehension, it is his neglect. The poem embodies a reproach, the wife/poet is being mistreated. As Freud suggests ('Mourning and Melancholia', pp. 260–1), the eventual target is not the poet's self but the neglectful Arthur, it is his fault. 'For him she plays, to him she sings/Of early faith and plighted vows' (97): why does she sing of these things? – because this may stir his conscience. And all this is subsequent to the trance of section 95: despite his visionary status, Arthur is still involved in the poet's fantasy in a tense interpersonal episode.

Explicitly, of course, the poet is inferior and deserted because Arthur is a soul in heaven. Tennyson commented on section 97: 'The relation of one on earth to one in the other and higher world. Not my relation to him here. He looked up to me as I looked up to him' (Ricks, *Poems*, p. 949). Nevertheless, it is my belief that what is exposed through Tennyson's preoccupation with Arthur's superior and neglectful stance is the continuation of a pattern of relations between the two young men which was established while Arthur was alive. Their admiration may indeed have been mutual, but Tennyson may have felt, even so, that he was dependent on the attention of his sophisticated, charismatic and popular friend. There is more than a touch of condescension in this letter from Arthur Hallam: 'I feel to-night what I own has been too uncommon with me of late, a strong desire to write to you. I do own I feel the want of you at some times more than at others; a sort of yearning for dear old Alfred comes upon

me, and that without any particularly apparent reason'
(*Memoir*, p. 87).

In section 42 the poet more or less admits the inequality
in the relationship:

> He still outstript me in the race;
>   It was but unity of place
> That made me dream I ranked with him.

Death rendered Arthur remote, lost, beyond communication, and made it possible for that to be considered
openly – through the discourse of death and heaven. But for
Tennyson there had always been the sense that their
commitment was not quite equal. Section 60 allows such an
extrapolation:

> He past; a soul of nobler tone:
>   My spirit loved and loves him yet,
>   Like some poor girl whose heart is set
> On one whose rank exceeds her own.
>
> He mixing with his proper sphere,
>   She finds the baseness of her lot,
>   Half jealous of she knows not what,
> And envying all that meet him there.

'Loved and loves' (in the second line) allows us to take the
analogue of the 'poor girl' as referring to the past as well as
the present relationship, and then the second stanza alludes
not only to Arthur's heavenly friends but to friends in his
lifetime – friends who Tennyson perhaps experienced as
more sophisticated intellectually, more amusing, and of a
higher social class. Section 110 discusses directly the poet's
exclusion from debates when Arthur was alive (he is on the
margin again):

> While I, thy nearest, sat apart,
>   And felt thy triumph was as mine;
>   And loved them more, that they were thine,
> The graceful tact, the Christian art;

> Nor mine the sweetness or the skill,
>> But mine the love that will not tire,
>> And, born of love, the vague desire
> That spurs an imitative will.

Perhaps it was rather trying for Arthur, aware of Tennyson trying to efface himself, gazing at him from the edge of the group, full of 'vague desire' which Arthur knew not quite how to meet. Tennyson's anxiety was still playing around this scene in 1875 when he printed 'nearest' (in the first line quoted) instead of 'dearest'.

It is the indirection of the death and heaven discourse which renders guilty and embarrassing what might have passed as intimacy – the sense that there is something which the poet cannot quite say in the existing languages of gender and sexuality. Ideas of death and heaven enabled him to construct certain feelings, but they fail to contain them – as the discourses of the love elegy and the domestic analogue fail. Repeatedly Tennyson seems to say both more and less than is appropriate, and if we allow ourselves to hear these dissonances customary notions of masculinity are confused and violated.

Whilst complaining at the reluctance of criticism to confront the genuinely challenging features of *In Memoriam*, it must be acknowledged that Tennyson himself helps to close them down. Towards the end of the poem the languages of love poetry and death and heaven move into a quasi-mystical register, which makes it far less important that Arthur was a real man – even suggests that he might be the same as Jesus.

> Known and unknown; human, divine;
>> Sweet human hand and lips and eye;
>> Dear heavenly friend that canst not die,
> Mine, mine, for ever, ever mine.

> (section 129)

The second line is perhaps disturbingly physical but it is buried in the abstraction and religiosity around it, and the urgency of the last line lacks a secure referent. And the family analogue is placed, for those who find the move convincing, by the epilogue and its celebration of a 'real' marriage. The domestic image finally domesticates, the ground of disturbance becomes the ground of incorporation. To use my earlier terms, the marginal emotional disturbance is reassimilated to the ideology of the centre.

At the same time, Arthur, as Eagleton has pointed out, is given a masculine identity as the statesman who will control the lower classes ('Politics and sexuality', p. 105). Even here, however, Tennyson manages a subtle slant: the love of bourgeois freedom is accompanied in Arthur by 'manhood fused with female grace' (p. 109). The idea of some convergence of feminine and masculine attributes is carried over from *The Princess*, and offered either as a resolution of the gender disturbance in the poem or, possibly, as a reminder of it. That *In Memoriam* retains considerable resistance to closure in matters of gender is manifest in the over-strenuous attempt of Kingsley to co-opt the poem for Christian manliness; he ended his review:

> Blessed, thrice blessed, to find that hero-worship is not yet passed away; that the heart of man still beats young and fresh; that the old tales of David and Jonathan, Damon and Pythias, Socrates and Alcibiades, Shakespeare and his nameless friend, of 'love passing the love of woman', ennobled by its own humility, deeper than death, and mightier than the grave, can still blossom out if it be but in one heart here and there to show men still how sooner or later 'he that loveth knoweth God, for God is Love!'
> (*Critical Heritage*, p. 185)

Kingsley risks a lot here, but hopes, evidently, that the sweep from boy scouts (so to speak) to 'God is Love' will somehow render all right the tricky implications of Greek love and Shakespeare's Sonnets. It is a bold but necessary move.

The adventurous nature of *In Memoriam* may be observed also, sadly, in Tennyson's anxieties about it – for instance some of the changes and glosses I have already discussed. 'If any body thinks I ever called him "dearest" in his life they are much mistaken, for I never even called him "dear"', Tennyson told Knowles in 1870–1 (Shatto and Shaw, *In Memoriam*, p. 232). In 1885, at a time of general public nervousness about the fall of Khartoum, renewed socialist agitation and the prospect of Home Rule for Ireland, and after a series of scandals, the Labouchère Amendment made *all* male homosexual acts illegal.[55] Tennyson was writing 'Locksley Hall Sixty Years After' (published 1886), and changed the line 'As our greatest is man-woman, so was she the woman-man' to 'She with all the charm of woman, she with all the breadth of man' (line 48). So he removed the idea of interchangeability and omitted altogether the idea that 'our greatest is man-woman'. In 1889 he wrote one of his most objectionable poems, four lines 'On One Who Affected an Effeminate Manner':

> While man and woman still are incomplete,
> I prize that soul where man and woman meet,
> Which types all Nature's male and female plan,
> But, friend, man-woman is not woman-man.

'Friend' in the last line is patronising in the immediate context, but resonant if we think of its frequent use in *In Memoriam*.

Tennyson's wish to distance himself from the effeminacy which previously he had dared is not just the retreat of an old man. Allon White has argued that from about the 1880s 'the relations between text, author and reader, swiftly changed'; it became 'less and less a case of looking at [literary] texts as either a reflection of the truth or an illuminating source throwing light upon it, but a case of looking through the semi-transparency of the words to the "real origin" which was the psycho-physiology of the author.'[56] Such 'symptomatic reading' subjected Tennyson's poems to questions he had not anticipated, and later writers learnt to cultivate a defensive indirection. *In Memoriam* is a poem of its time not just in the anxieties about science and revolution, but in its whole construction of sexuality and self. Its blurring of gender divisions offers to the modern reader a challenge which later writers could hardly envisage, let alone sustain.

6   The Laureate in the Market Place

Poetry and Class

I suggested at the start of the previous chapter that Tennyson intuited in the writing of *In Memoriam* a way of negotiating difficulties in the role ascribed to poetry in his time. The reception of the poem confirmed him in this belief, and the consequent conferral of the laureateship gave him a sense of official and public approbation. Now his name gained a purchase in reality far beyond that afforded by the waking trance he induced by repeating his name to himself. He had begun to have meaning for others, as an important token in the construction of Literature within the Victorian cultural apparatus. Valerie Pitt has given the most sympathetic and astute account of what it meant to Tennyson to be laureate:

> It was, like his marriage, an element in his new psychological stability – a link which bound him to the world of affairs. To be the ceremonial voice of the State, the servant of its Servant, was to have status in the community, and what is more, a status, not merely as a person, but as a poet: there was no need to deny the inner voice or the solitary vision. . . . The Bard, the Laureate, is the prophet as well as the priest of the community, the *Vates* who sees deep into the realities of the spiritual and moral life, and is capable of revealing to society the state of its own soul.[1]

The process described here seems to heal the breach in the poet's mission which occurred when Shelley's combination of imaginative and political liberty was abandoned. The poet gains a new authority as the bard who speaks for the people, but now the interests of the people are defined by the state rather than through identification with those oppressed by the state. And, as Valerie Pitt indicates, the laureate has a link with 'the world of affairs', though his particular contribution is to do with spiritual and moral life. So the depiction of states of mind, at which Tennyson was certainly experienced, is found to be of national importance. Proposing a health to Tennyson in 1883, Gladstone compared himself: 'he has worked in a higher field, and his work will be more durable'[2] – this is the assumption through which the state kept poetry out of politics. The laureate is official keeper of the margins.

Commentators have sometimes presented Tennyson as a poet who sold out in order to adjust to the taste and concerns of his age. But such adjustment could not easily be made. The public was remote and its culture was not homogeneous: it was difficult to know how diverse sections would react to this or that poem. The reception of Tennyson after 1850 was a sequence of surprises and disappointments for the aspiring bard.[3] The problem is manifest in the way Tennyson used reading aloud to friends. Not only was this a preliminary to publication, with the hope of anticipating criticism; also Tennyson at every opportunity read aloud published poems – for the reason that they 'would lose much of their force without the proper cadence imparted by impassioned reading'.[4] Tennyson was trying to restore a face to face relationship with a readership which was remote – as Samuel Johnson's and even Shelley's was not. Geoffrey Best describes 'the decisive creation, during our period [1851–70], of a mass-market for cheap literature'.[5] Tennyson could not anticipate the conditions of reception.

He was writing for an unprecedentedly huge readership: *Enoch Arden* in 1864 sold 17,000 on the day of publication,

40,000 within three months, 60,000 within five months; in 1869 26,000 copies of *The Holy Grail* were ordered before publication.[6] But it was all out of control, beyond reach, and reading aloud was an attempt to get at least a few hearers to receive the poem in the way Tennyson meant it. He was particularly anxious about the unpopularity of *Maud*. Hallam Tennyson's *Memoir* records, without seeing the significance: 'It is notable that two such appreciative critics as Mr Gladstone and Dr Van Dyke wholly mis-apprehended the meaning of "Maud" until they heard my father read it, and that they both then publicly recanted their first criticisms' (p. 336). I argued in chapter 4 that Tennyson's use of prefaces and frameworks manifests his anxiety about communicating: he could not rely on a remote readership. There was a further convolution in the split between private reading and public endorsement, for eventually one came to interfere with the other. Martin remarks: 'the more famous he became the more he was in demand to read, but the more he read the more he needed to believe that he was being praised for the intrinsic worth of the poetry not for the fame of the poet' (*Tennyson*, p. 407). The name which seemed to establish the integrity of his self and of his poetry took on its own momentum.

The mass market was not just an inconvenience. It was the necessary ratification of the bardic enterprise. The laureateship might seem to guarantee public status, but in practice it was far too nebulous to sustain Tennyson's writing. The final estimate of significance in a market economy can be nothing other than sales. As Marx and Engels remarked, 'The bourgeoisie has stripped of its halo every occupation hitherto honoured and looked up to with reverent awe. It has converted the physician, the lawyer, the priest, the poet, the man of science, into its paid wage labourers.'[7] Tennyson worried about his sales and drove hard bargains with publishers. In 1868 J. Bertrand Payne tried to jostle him into a standard edition and he grumbled: 'I expect now that if I do not publish this edition (and I have little desire to do it) the sales of the old one will fall off

in expectation of this'; his wife complained, revealingly:
'What I do really care for is that my Ally should stand
before the world in his own child-like simplicity and by this
he would be made to appear a more cunning tradesman'
(Hagen, *Publishers*, p. 117). Tennyson's reaction was a
cunning enough piece of trading – he changed his publisher: Alexander Strahan agreed to buy the copyright of
existing poems for a period of five years for £5,000 annually,
and to pay ten per cent on the proceeds from new work
(Tennyson insisted on this latter). So Tennyson was almost
a salaried writer; in 1873 he struck a similar deal with
Henry King (Hagen, *Publishers*, pp. 117, 133–4). Strung out
between a few individual auditors and the remote public, it
seemed natural to estimate success by sales and income. In
1859 George Smith wanted to commission another book of
Idylls like that just published; Tennyson exclaimed jovially
to his wife: 'My dear! We are much richer than we thought
we were. Mr Smith has just offered me five thousand
guineas for a book the size of the "Idylls". And, if Mr Smith
offers five thousand, of course the book is worth ten'
(Martin, *Tennyson*, p. 424). That is how 'worth' is estimated
in a capitalist society.

The further problem was that the public was not uniform
– in fact the term 'public' is a construction of market
economics. The appearance of homogeneity is an effect of
ideology – it obscures the divergence of interests of different
classes and class fractions. This ideological effect was
relatively successful at the time when Tennyson became
laureate. Geoffrey Best agrees that there was indeed a
mid-Victorian calm – from about 1850, when the disturbances of 1848 seemed to have passed off safely, perhaps as
far on as the early seventies: 'Not only did Britain
unmistakably lead the world in commerce and manufactures, she was held to lead also in setting an example of a
harmonious and orderly modern society that needed no, so
to speak, "external", imposed-by-government military or
police power to keep order, but kept order of its own
accord.'[8] People of all classes were persuaded to believe

that the current order was necessary, in their interests, or both. There was wide assent to the importance of independence and respectability; key concepts, elaborated by Bagehot, were 'deference' and 'removable inequalities'. So people were reconciled to the current order. As Palmerston put it in a famous speech of 1850: 'every class of society accepts with cheerfulness the lot which providence has assigned to it; while at the same time each individual of each class is constantly trying to raise himself in the social scale, not by violence and illegality, but by persevering good conduct and by the steady and energetic exertion of the moral and intellectual faculties with which his creator has endowed him' (quoted by Best, p. 255).

Despite this appearance, several factors manifested the actual complexity of the social formation and rendered problematic the bardic role of the poet. First, despite assertions of shared values, poetry was read mainly by the middle classes – they were the people who could afford to buy it. Altick observes: 'By 1850 about 110,000 families had an annual income of over £150. Of these, by far the greater portion belonged to the middle or lower-middle class. . . . These families, willing to spend five or six shillings on a book but seldom more, constituted the prime market for cheap books.' (This was at a time when 'London shipwrights made 36s. a week, builder's labourers 20s. Ironfounders had a weekly wage of 27s.6d. The average weekly wage in the Lancashire and Cheshire cotton factories was only 9s.6d.')[9] The market for books grew considerably in the third quarter of the century and circulating libraries made them cheaply available, but the conditions for the production of poetry had been set. Monckton Milnes represents excellently the confident phase of bourgeois hegemony in his assertion, in a review of Tennyson's *Poems* (1842), that the poet is now free from aristocratic patronage and hence 'enjoys the dignity and is subject to the responsibilities of independence' – having to sell one's wares did not seem to Milnes a constraint. And this was very good for poetry:

Among the large and intelligent middle classes of this country there is much poetry read and enjoyed. . . . Take up any magazine, and see not only how comparatively high is the general character of its poetry in diction and execution, but how healthy even its commonplaces are, how reflective or affectionate or pious, how free from appeals to the baser passions and the lower conditions of our nature. (*Critical Heritage*, pp. 137–8)

The irony and awkwardness of this cultural formation should not be overlooked. As Jane P. Tompkins puts it, 'the audience for literature in the nineteenth century was the new urban middle class, enriched by the industrial developments that the Romantic and Victorian poets feared and condemned.'[10] Tennyson as much as anyone had expressed his ambivalence towards utilitarianism, political economy and machinery, but he was obliged to construe the bardic role in terms set by the class which lived by them.

Middle-class domination of poetry promoted certain limitations on the subjects and manner of the bard's prophecies. A principal objection to *Maud* was its social and political comment. Coventry Patmore declared, 'The fever of politics should not have been caught by the Laureate even under the disguise of a monomaniac';[11] the *Manchester Examiner and Times* castigated explicitly the 'lying libel upon trade and the trading community', insisting that peace had filled the land 'with monuments of our skill and enterprise till the nation had almost lost its warlike instincts in the humanizing pursuits of trade'.[12] Robert Martin believes that Gladstone's rebuke over 'Locksley Hall Sixty Years After' – that it marred the Queen's jubilee with 'tragic notes' – was 'a long-delayed rebuke to Tennyson for meddling with public affairs' (*Tennyson*, p. 561). Instead poetry, and the laureate's especially, was supposed to deal with alleged general principles and emotions of humanity. This is what Gladstone admired in *Idylls of the King* in 1859: 'It is national: it is Christian. It is also human in the largest and deepest sense; and, therefore, though highly national, it is universal; for it rests upon those depths and breadths of our nature to which all its truly great developments in all nations are alike essentially and closely related.'[13] The absolutizing of local values, a primary strategy of ideology, could hardly be better illustrated: national → Christian → human → universal. *Maud*, conversely, was distrusted for embracing a minority state of feeling – the poet, Bagehot complained, 'seemed to sympathize with the feverish railings, the moody nonsense, the very entangled philosophy, which he put into the mouth of his hero' (*Critical Heritage*, p. 219). As I showed in chapter 2, this was John Wilson's argument in 1830: unorthodox states of mind threaten to undermine the necessity of normality.

Poetry might take up tricky issues – P. G. Scott has shown that the subject of remarriage, in *Enoch Arden*, was one such. But in the handling, John Killham points out, no account is taken of 'legal complications, metaphysical speculations or for that matter, actual circumstances of class, poverty and sexual attraction': it is all reduced to faith and morals, corresponding to a preference for 'a literature which avoided the unpleasant realities of life or if it did not, made them simple moral issues'.[14] The contrasting critical reactions to *Maud* in 1855 and *Idylls of the King* in 1859 encapsulate these bourgeois preferences. Bagehot deprecated in *Maud* 'some odd invectives against peace, against industry, against making your livelihood' whereas the *Idylls* show 'the trace of a very mature judgment' – here 'Mr Tennyson has sided with the world' (*Critical Heritage*, pp. 219–20). Gladstone made the same contrast; the suffocating pressure to speak for a middle-class norm is well illustrated in Gladstone's insistence that Tennyson was really one of them all along: he is 'too intimately and essentially the poet of the nineteenth century to separate himself from its leading characteristics, the progress of physical science and a vast commercial, mechanical and industrial development' (*Critical Heritage*, p. 248). Tennyson couldn't really mean what he seemed to be saying in *Maud*.

The determination with which bourgeois ideology was being pressed upon the laureate should not lead us to assume that it was entirely secure – perhaps the opposite; it is the function of ideology to obscure conflict and contradiction. Three further factors complicated the configuration of class attitudes to which poetry was expected to be responsive. First, it was widely believed that the lower classes would be more docile if they were incorporated into bourgeois culture, and poetry was expected to assist. Matthew Arnold in 'Democracy' argued that middle-class culture must maintain a 'grandeur of spirit', otherwise it 'will almost certainly fail to mould or assimilate the masses below'.[15] F. W. Robertson told a meeting at a Mechanics' Institute that poetry can 'enable the man of labour to rise sometimes out of his dull, dry, hard toil, and dreary routine of daily life, into forgetfulness of his state, to breathe a higher and serener, and purer atmosphere'.[16] Hence Gladstone's lasting reservation about *Maud*, as to 'whether it is to be desired that a poem should require from common men a good deal of effort in order to comprehend it' (*Memoir*, p. 336).

Tennyson certainly felt that he should contribute to the process of 'humanizing' (i.e. making unaware of their oppression) the lower classes. He arranged for 10,000 copies of his 'Ode on the Death of the Duke of Wellington' (1851) to be printed and sold at two shillings to the crowd at the funeral – though he preferred Moxon's two shillings with £200 for himself to John Parker's one shilling with £150 for himself (Martin, *Tennyson*, p. 368). He wanted people to be told 'On God and Godlike men we build our trust' (line 266). In 1864 'he made up his mind to issue a selection of the more popular of his poems in sixpenny parts, hoping that these would reach the working men of England.'[17] But his publisher thought this wouldn't be profitable, so they settled for a more ornamental one-volume edition at five shillings. In 1870 Alexander Strahan proposed another cheap edition – his ambition was clearly expressed: 'Furnish the people liberally with literature. . . .

We shall find that in the writings of our best authors we possess all we require to strike our grappling-iron into the working people's soul, and chain them, willing followers, to the car of advancing civilization' (Hagen, *Publishers*, p. 122). However, Strahan's business failed before the scheme could be implemented. In each of these projects the shuffle between ideological and commercial motives is fascinating to observe.

Plainly people of all classes did read Tennyson's poems – not because he represented universal values, but because he was contributing to the process by which aspiring and deferential lower classes were incorporated into and rendered subject to bourgeois hegemony. G. M. Young's impression is instructive:

> imagine yourself to be one of its [*Enoch Arden*'s] 60,000 purchasers: or better still, perhaps, sitting in the village schoolroom to hear it read by the vicar or the squire. What do you find? An abundance, a vast profusion of poetic learning, of ornate phrasing and verbal music – which you will recognize and admire, because it is the familiar accent of Tennyson, though in detail much of it may be above your head – applied to a tale of common life lived on the heroic level.[18]

The vicar and the squire might indeed wish people thus impressed and subdued.

Young's remark about life at a heroic level leads towards a second complication in bourgeois hegemony, namely the continuing admiration for nobility of birth. Geoffrey Best comments: 'The aristocracy was irresistibly fascinating to a historically- and hierarchically-minded, socially ambitious and envious society, because its members seemed to be *heroic*. They were supposed to look handsomer, love more passionately and behave more impressively than lower-bred mortals' (*Mid-Victorian Britain*, p. 266). This was the pinnacle of the pyramid of deference which kept most Victorians from aspiring too far above their places. Despite the vigour with which the bourgeoisie dominated industrial and commercial relations and imposed their culture on the nation, they retained as a glittering instance of true nobility the idea of aristocratic birth. Monckton Milnes acknowledged this factor in literary life, though he believed it to be only a residue, when he said: 'London lionism still remains, – the last stage of that condescension of ignorance and folly to wisdom and knowledge, by which wealth and power flatter themselves into the notion that they have something to give' (*Critical Heritage*, p. 137).

The elegant salons to which Milnes was referring did not die out, however, they increased in importance. Tennyson was sucked into this world from the mid-fifties. At Little Holland House Mrs Prinsep and her six sisters kept court; Martin says they were 'rich, exuberant, intelligent, eccentric, and all but one of them were beautiful' (*Tennyson*, p. 407), but that is perhaps to take them at the valuation of the time: in any event, they were rich. So they married aristocrats and Tennyson, along with Burne-Jones, Holman Hunt, Rossetti, Woolner, George Eliot, Thackeray, Thomas Hughes, the Brownings and Patmore, gave a literary-artistic cachet to their Sunday at-homes. Tennyson's capacity to be impressed by such people is sadly documented; it went along with his readiness to accept the phoney pedigree his uncle had commissioned and to claim descent from the Plantagenets (Martin, *Tennyson*, pp. 402, 412–13, 377–8, 543–4). Of course, he was not a conventional guest, but a certain shagginess of appearance and behaviour was quite in order if one was a great poet. Martin observes: 'It would be wrong to suggest that all his noble acquaintances thought of him as a social curiosity' (*Tennyson*, p. 413), but for many that is what he was, a kind of elephant man.

Tennyson's personal involvement in the patterns of deference which sustained a social hierarchy and, to a degree, masked the realities of power, only marks him as a man of his time – along with many others of note. But it may also lead us to expect a certain asymmetry in the relation between his writing and the hegemonic class. At the risk of being simplistic, I would derive part of the appeal of *Idylls of the King* in Victorian culture from its compatibility with the aristocratic display which was admired in that culture. The 'heroic' action Young remarked in *Enoch Arden* was boldly conceived in so far as it involved lowly persons – hence Bagehot's sense of inappropriateness at the 'varnish' applied to the 'horrid' Enoch to make him 'shine' (see p. 84 above). The shining of the *Idylls* seems of a piece with the characters and settings; but it is also remarkably compatible with the function of upper-class display in Victorian ideology: Best explains, drawing on Bagehot's analysis:

> while political power really rested in the hands of the middle classes (themselves, of course, rather deferential too), the masses were deferring not to them but to 'what we may call the *theatrical show* of society ... a certain pomp of great men; a certain spectacle of beautiful women; a wonderful scene of wealth and enjoyment ... a certain charmed spectacle which imposes on the many, and guides their fancies as it will'.[19]

For those who could not get to central London to gaze at the great men and beautiful women in their charmed spectacle, *Idylls of the King* may have proved an acceptable substitute – a comparable distraction from the realities of power.

A third factor which complicated the bourgeois poet's relationship with his public was the development within the middle class of a distinctive fraction or category of intellectuals. In the mid-Victorian period, T. W. Heyck explains, 'most men of letters did share fundamental middle-class values and concerns. They shared with their audience the ideals of social relations and public order'.[20] This is the spirit in which the 1859 *Idylls* were conceived and received. But the mass market and the significant role of cultural production as a hegemonic force operating through it, even while they encouraged identification with popular values, at the same time led to an increasing specialization and self-consciousness among writers, scholars, scientists, artists and thinkers. As Heyck puts it, the development was from men of letters to intellectuals. Literature had concerned itself since the late eighteenth century with a critique of the ideology of industry and commerce and, as I showed in chapter 2, Arthur Hallam set out the idea of an autonomous role for poetry, validated through its opposition to everyday experience. This possibility was rejected by the mid-Victorian person of letters – Bagehot regretted that Tennyson's early writing had been under the immature influence of young men 'of rather heated imaginations' (*Critical Heritage*, p. 217). In its most expansive phase, bourgeois hegemony appropriated almost entirely the concept of poetry, it was incorporated. But from about 1870 writers and thinkers took up the Hallam line, manifesting 'a reaction against the values of the middle-class reader and a revulsion from a new audience with which they had little contact or sympathy'. So 'intellectuals' as we think of them appeared – detached, alienated even; an elite distinct from the central hierarchy of power in the society, eager 'to break away from a market relation with their publics in order to pursue some kind of self-validating scholarship or art' (Heyck, pp. 177, 182).

The consequence was a swing in Tennyson's reputation – Isobel Armstrong describes it as a complete reversal of the criteria of praise and blame (*Victorian Scrutinies*, pp. 53–9). As early as 1864 Swinburne was complaining privately of sanctimony in Tennyson's poetry and Meredith of sentimentalization,[21] and the *British Review* observed that 'the age governs Mr Tennyson's utterances, which are the accepted expression of its complex fashions.'[22] The new breed of intellectuals valued challenge rather than conformity. Now uncommon psychological states were prized – Armstrong shows John Morley's defence of *The Ring and the Book* to be based on 'the *extension* and expansion of the sympathies. He is not thinking of the *consolidation*' demanded in earlier decades (p. 58). And the *British Quarterly Review* in 1870 regretted Tennyson's tendency to console: 'he skirts the margin of the darkest places of modern doubt and difficulty, and faithfully overseeing them, yet returns with the image of a fairer reality' (Armstrong, p. 315). These commentators were all concerned to separate themselves from common opinion – Alfred Austin began his attack on Tennyson in 1870 with the proposition that 'in the formation of opinion . . . the conventional sense of the majority . . . overpowers the critical sense of the discriminating minority' (*Critical Heritage*, p. 294).

In other words, what the poet was expected to do changed beneath Tennyson as he wrote. Having been encouraged by Hallam to cultivate a special poetic sensitivity, he had managed nevertheless in *In Memoriam* to negotiate current expectations to the extent that he seemed the appropriate laureate. Then as he tried to take up the bardic role, the exclusive sensibility of the poet was reasserted by a new generation of alienated intellectuals, reacting against the very public which had demanded Tennyson's allegiance. No wonder he was so angry at one of their slogans: 'Art for Art's sake! Hail, truest lord of Hell!', he wrote in 1869. Yet he had always been anxious about the conditions of writing under bourgeois hegemony. In 1866 he said to William Allingham: 'Why am I popular? I don't write very vulgarly.'[23] We may see here a glimmer of the feeling identified by Sartre as that of the writer in the second half of the nineteenth century: 'he sold his productions, but he despised those who bought them.'[24] Tennyson was transitional and deeply split: he believed that his work could best be validated by a mass public, but engaged in private reading whenever he could. Perhaps at a deep level he came to despise his readers. Certainly we may intuit in *Maud* an ambivalence towards the prevailing conditions of literary production.

The Excessiveness of Maud

I do not intend to follow through Tennyson's later career; in many respects he continued with earlier practices and

concerns, and I have discussed 'The Ancient Sage', 'Far –
Far – Away', *Enoch Arden* and 'In the Valley of Cauteretz'.
Nor do I intend to try to substantiate in detail the
inferences I have drawn about *Idylls of the King* – that they
effected, by and large, a negotiation of middle-class
demands upon the laureate so safe that the intellectuals of
that class rejected it. This would be a large and melancholy
task, and I doubt that the poem's enthusiasts would be
convinced. To be sure, the *Idylls* may be read to disclose
structural contradictions[25] (what may not?), but such
disturbances are manifest in *Maud* and that is the case
which stimulates consideration. In it Tennyson stretches
almost all the concepts this study has so far applied to him.

Maud was notoriously unpopular: George Eliot saw in it
'scarcely more than a residuum of Alfred Tennyson; the
wide-sweeping intellect, the mild philosophy, the healthy
pathos, the wondrous melody, have almost all vanished'.
The *New Quarterly Review* was representative: 'we miss
altogether the sweetness and music which elsewhere
distinguish Mr Tennyson's poetry. We miss that delicacy
and maturity of thought, that elaboration and completeness
of form, which render absolutely perfect of its kind much of
what he has already achieved in song.'[26] In this instance
either Tennyson did not want to be the poet of his
bourgeois public, or he tried but failed, or both motives
were confusingly present at once.

Maud confronts the middle class on its own ground; there
is no glamour of knights and ladies or distant voyages. Its
exotic aspects are all in the unstable personality of the
speaker. Despite this – and it is a provocative juxtaposition
– the speaker is fully implicated in the bourgeois order. His
father and Maud's made money through speculative
trading, and he is just on the edge of those who can be
publicly acknowledged by the family at the hall (compare
Tennyson's relations with his grandfather and uncle – p. 21
above). His criticism of how wealth and status are distri-
buted is from the inside. Yet he is poor enough to make the
idea of marriage with Maud problematic; and that idea is

problematized still further by the possibility of inherited madness. Foucault has pointed out the bourgeoisie's pre-occupation with 'the menaces of heredity; families wore and concealed a sort of reversed and somber escutcheon whose defamatory quarters were the diseases or defects of the group of relatives.'[27] In Ibsen's *Ghosts*, for instance, this becomes the ground for a curse on the house analogous to the blood-feuding in Greek tragedy. Health and wealth combine to impede the marriage of the speaker and Maud, and to render him a disturbing presence within the middle class.

All this might be adequately resolved by the death of the major parties, including perhaps the speaker in the war, if the mode of the poem permitted narrative closure. But a primary issue is the status of the speaker – his enthusiasm for the Crimean War makes it unavoidable. Gladstone wrote in 1859: 'We finally own that our divining rod does not enable us to say whether the poet intends to be in any and what degree sponsor to these sentiments' (*Critical Heritage*, p. 247).

I argued in chapter 4 that the refusal of dramatic monologue to allow the reader to rest confidently in the notion of the coherent, autonomous human subject – its refusal to settle for either a first- or third-person voice – offers a major obstacle to the ruling practices of conventional criticism. *Maud* has been found problematic because it offers a powerful challenge to customary ideas of the relationship between author, text and reader. One consequent critical strategy is an insistence on the dramatic aspect of the poem and the construction of a unity on this assumption. A skilful instance is John Killham's essay; Ann C. Colley in a recent book takes a similar line.[28] Another strategy is to insist on the lyric aspect and propose 'Tennyson' as the essential self behind the text – for a sensible account of the personal pressures on Tennyson see Ricks' chapter on the poem; at a further extreme the poem has attracted psychoanalytic attention.[29] Or one may admit defeat – or, rather, declare the poem defective: Ricks and

Philip Drew register its indeterminate voice and imply that it is a flaw.[30]

The indeterminacy is evidently related to issues discussed earlier in this chapter: Tennyson had trouble reading his readers and could not fix the relationship between them and himself. On the one hand he asserted that the speaker of *Maud* is an invention, as often in dramatic poems: 'they often only express a poetic instinct, or judgment on character real or imagined, and on the facts of lives real or imagined'; he encouraged Robert Mann to write about the poem in this vein.[31] On the other hand, he did not want to relinquish control of his work: he read *Maud* aloud as often as he could, believing that the true feeling of the poem would be communicated by him personally – 'You were at once put in sympathy with the hero', his son said of the last reading in 1892 (*Memoir*, p. 334). The divided subject position of the speaker corresponds to Tennyson's own.

Simply to celebrate *Maud* as a rendering of a dispersed subject would not take us far beyond reversing the categories of conventional criticism. The poem is so peculiar, and Tennyson's relationship with it was so intense, that it demands a more material analysis in terms of the divergent pressures in the whole construction of Victorian culture. The obvious point to make is that Tennyson was uncertain how far he wanted to press social and political criticism of the prevailing order. The poor are hustled together in hovels, wine and bread are adulterated, machinery grinds through the night, poisons are dispensed as medicines, children are murdered for burial fees – and all because 'only the ledger lives' (I, 35, and 34–45). These are serious charges, and of course they were all true. If Tennyson does not mean to press them, I would say, he should not use them for dramatic effect or the sake of the story. Yet they are placed in the mouth of a speaker who admits his own imbalance: 'What! am I raging alone as my father raged in his mood?' (I, 53; Tennyson added this in 1856 to distance himself from the speaker). The poem plays across Tennyson's anxieties about bourgeois freedom but hesitates to close in on fundamental injustices with conviction. This was not a new tendency: 'Locksley Hall', which I discussed in chapter 2, does much the same thing. But the issues are sharper once he is laureate, for he is supposed to speak for the establishment. He can neither repudiate nor accept the marginal voice of the speaker in *Maud*.

What is so striking about *Maud* and its hostile reception is that it was Tennyson's next major poem after the publication of *In Memoriam*, general approbation for which caused him to be made laureate, and in many ways it seems designed as a follow-up. It consists of a sequence of reflections and emotional states, given in short sections which the reader is expected to connect up; the development is from gloom and instability to personal faith and faith in the future of England; the key to this is an experience of love and loss – this time, reassuringly one presumes, the love is heterosexual; and the loss is partly retrieved through a visionary trance in which the beloved says that all may yet be well ('She seemed to divide in a dream from a band of the blest,/And spoke of a hope for the world in the coming wars', III, 10–11). So from this basis the speaker feels able to offer generalizations about the virtues of bourgeois freedom, setting the imaginative intensity of his personal experience against mechanistic ideas of humanity. It is all very like *In Memoriam* and the language, again, is densely structured and poetic: it claims the fulness of presence which appears to close the gap between sign and referent, and discovers in Maud and then in 'the purpose of God, and the doom assigned' (III, 59) a transcendental signified – the impossible Other which, like Arthur, dies and yet persists, which beckons from a future which probably (as in *In Memoriam* and 'Ulysses') holds the speaker's death.

This is what is so interesting about *Maud*: Tennyson seems in a way to make all the right moves, but yet the result is strange and was to many initial readers unacceptable. It is as if he were taking the dominant construction of poetry and his own skill at negotiating it, and pushing it all one stage further – confronting it with itself and challenging it to acknowledge itself. At every point *Maud* offers an excess, a surplus of effect which calls into question the principles by which it purports to exist and have meaning.

In the approach I have associated with Tennyson, poetic language is supposed to be excessive: that is how it suggests its own special density, particularly through symbolic writing – the blurring of literal and figurative so as to postulate an identification between the self and the world via language. In *Maud* this process is self-consciously extreme and perverse. The comment in *Blackwood's Magazine* in 1856 makes the point: 'When we feel Nature sympathising with us, it is well; but it is not well when we force her to echo our own mad fancies, of themselves forced and unreal enough.'[32] At the start of the following lines, for instance, the speaker seems to know the difference between the world and his emotions, but within a short space he converts the landscape into a reflection of his preoccupations:

> ah, wherefore cannot I be
> Like things of the season gay, like the beautiful season
>   bland,
> When the far-off sail is blown by the breeze of a softer
>   clime,
> Half-lost in the liquid azure bloom of a crescent of sea,
> The silent sapphire-spangled marriage ring of the
>   land?
>
> (I, 103–7)

The symbolic merging of mind and landscape should be consoling, a pleasant delusion of or nostalgia for unity of being. Tennyson in *Maud* pushes it to the point where it denies that comfort. Again, earlier in the same section he dreams of Maud, 'Luminous, gemlike, ghostlike, deathlike' (I, 95) – understandably strange and spooky, being a dream. But when, waking, he describes what was actually there in the garden, four lines later, it is even more weird and informed with nuances evidently deriving from the speaker's psychological condition. He listened

> to the scream of a maddened beach dragged
> down by the wave,
> Walked in a wintry wind by a ghastly glimmer, and
> found
> The shining daffodil dead, and Orion low in his grave.
>
> (I, 99–101)

The language of personal feeling and the sudden intense concentration on disparate details make it difficult to distinguish the external world from the poet's mind.

This symbolic effect is disconcerting, and the mind which presumably governs it is strange and unstable. This is apparent also in abrupt shifts of level, for instance in these lines from 'Come into the garden, Maud': the rivulet falls

> From the meadow your walks have left so sweet
>   That whenever a March-wind sighs
> He sets the jewel-print of your feet
>   In violets blue as your eyes,
> To the woody hollows in which we meet
>   And the valleys of Paradise.
>
> (I, 888–93)

The notion that the small flowers as they bow before the breeze are displaying a reminiscence of Maud's footprint is extravagant, but the acute visual perception reassures us that the speaker is in touch with the world. But 'valleys of Paradise' shifts into fantasy. Philip Drew makes a similar point about the move from this: 'the dry-tongued laurels' pattering talk/Seemed her light foot along the garden walk', which, again, is observed and aware – to this: 'The gates of Heaven are closed, and she is gone' (I, 606–7, 610).[33] These disconcerting disjunctions occur also around the biblical imagery which the speaker applies to Maud – for instance in these two lines:

> Your father is ever in London, you wander about at
>   your will;
> You have but fed on the roses and lain in the lilies of
>   life.
>
> (I, 160–1)

Imagery of lilies and roses, recalling the Song of Solomon, seems to be proposing Maud as a divine being, but the discontinuities around it call into question the reliability of that vision.

In 'Tithonus' the symbolic mode and the coherence of the speaker's subjectivity are brought into question by a sense that the world is determining the speaker rather than the other way about (pp. 108–9 above). In *Maud* the determination by the speaker is so manifest and arbitrary that the vision seems merely fantasy. The implications of this effect are far-reaching, for such density of language, I have shown, is integral to the nineteenth-century construction of poetry. Upon it rests the distinction between poetic and ordinary experience, which secures in one aspect poetry's authority and in another aspect its marginality. By connecting poetic strategies of presence to the mind of a disturbed person, Tennyson undermines the whole status of poetic vision. If this is not visionary but deranged –

> But the rose was awake all night for your sake,
>   Knowing your promise to me;
> The lilies and roses were all awake,
>   They sighed for the dawn and thee
>
> (I, 898–91)

(and it doesn't matter which we decide, for in a matter of such delicacy the question is enough, though many of Tennyson's contemporaries thought it deranged) – then why not this?:

> And all the breeze of Fancy blows,
>   And every dew-drop paints a bow,
>   The wizard lightnings deeply glow,
> And every thought breaks out a rose.
>
> (*In Memoriam*, 122)

The whole process, through which poetry claims to remedy the defect of ordinary language and heal the breach between humankind and reality, is in doubt. What comes under threat in *Maud* is the very heart of the current construction of poetry.

This precarious enterprise is in part an aggressive surfacing of disturbances, about sexuality and the class structure, which run all through Tennyson's poetry. More specifically, I attribute it to the laureateship and a consequent combination of *confidence* and *frustration*. Tennyson now thought he knew what was expected of him and how to do it; that was the confidence. The frustration I intuit from his perhaps submerged determination to follow *In Memoriam* with a poem which, while seeming to satisfy many of the current criteria, *actually* goes over the top and renders them problematic. It arose, I suggest, precisely from his sense that he was the laureate, popular, married, prosperous, competent. Aubrey de Vere told him in 1845, when he was grumbling about being constrained by growing old, lack of recognition, money and peace, that 'he wanted occupation, a wife, and orthodox principles.'[34] Now that he had these things, he found himself trapped by what was supposed to liberate him. The construction of poetry is also the construction of 'Tennyson'. *Maud* is the product of a writer who understands the game and resents it.

The one respect in which Tennyson might have doubted his capacity to please the public is manliness, and here perhaps he was least in conscious control of his project. As I showed in the previous chapter, *In Memoriam* is potentially subversive in its treatment of gender, and friendly commentators had to forestall criticism (he writes 'not in vain effeminate complaint', Gladstone asserted – *Critical Heritage*, p. 245). Here again, Tennyson adopts in *Maud* the recipe of his culture with such vigour that we should suspect an over-reaction. Maud is blatantly stereotyped, first as the fatal Cleopatra who 'meant to weave me a snare/Of some coquettish deceit' (I, 214–16), then at the other extreme as the heavenly maiden who is moved by talk of mothers (I, 701–16). Lionel Stevenson's view of this in 1948 was that as Tennyson 'gained emotional stability, he gradually transformed the mysterious maiden [of some early poems] into a matter-of-fact literary stock-character'.[35] I don't know whether Jungians other than Stevenson hold this lamentable conception of 'maturity' (p. 135); I would say that the stereotyping evidences gender insecurity, and other over-aggressive bits of 'masculinity' do the same. There is the rival lover, presented as effeminate – men 'soften' to him 'as if to a girl', he is

> a padded shape,
> A bought commission, a waxed face,
> A rabbit mouth that is ever agape.
>
> (I, 345, 358–60)

He is 'the babe-faced lord', 'the languid fool,/Who was gaping and grinning by' (II, 13, 19–20). Furthermore, the appearance of this rival provokes one of the speaker's main effusions on the desirability of war – he attacks Quakers as in the pay of cotton manufacturers, recalls Maud's 'chivalrous battle-song', doubts that she could 'take a wanton dissolute boy/For a man and leader of men', prays for a strong ruler, 'a man with heart, head, hand,/Like some of the simple great ones gone'. If only the speaker was confident and fulfilled in his own masculinity – 'And ah for a man to arise to me,/That the man I am may cease to be!' (I, 366–97). The idea of war, plainly, helps the speaker to feel masculine, and this is so transparent that, as with the excessive symbolic language, it brings its own ideological construction into visibility.

That the manly political posture was more for Tennyson than an immediate reaction to the Crimean War and more than a way of rounding off *Maud* can be seen from the fact that it appears also in political poems written in response to the coup d'état of Louis Napoleon in France in December 1851. These poems, Sir Charles Tennyson says, display 'an attitude towards national affairs entirely different to any

displayed by Tennyson before'.[36] English bourgeois free-
dom is evoked in the manner of the poems of 1831–3, with
some customary plundering of lines from 'Hail Briton!', but
the main burden is the need to arm and fight foreigners.
Tennyson published 'The Third of February, 1852' and
'Hands All Round!' in *The Examiner* over the pseudonym
'Merlin' (note the prophetic claim); and then over the
Welsh bardic name 'Taliessin', referring to those earlier
pieces, he published 'Suggested by Reading an Article in a
Newspaper'. It begins:

> How much I love this writer's manly style!
>   By such men led, our press had ever been
> The public conscience of our noble isle,
>   Severe and quick to feel a civic sin,
> To raise the people and chastise the times
> With such a heat as lives in great creative rhymes.

Here Tennyson is setting out what he evidently took to be a
laureate function, the role of the poet in recalling his society
to its best self; this is his attempt to retrieve the bardic
authority which had lapsed with the Shelleyan conjunction
of political and imaginative liberty. And it is *manly*: thus
Tennyson seeks to repudiate both the effeminacy and the
marginality with which poetry was involved, and his own
poetry specifically. 'Britons, Guard Your Own' begins:
'Rise, Britons, rise, if manhood be not dead'. Britain is
asserted as a centred unity over against the exteriority of
the French, and the poet is recentred as the bard of 'manly
style'.

The excessive masculinity of *Maud* exposes the contradictions of this project: like the excessive symbolic language, it
presses so hard upon the hegemonic construction of poetry
that it loses credibility. The speaker's bellicosity and actual
fighting seemed to many readers hysterical and the war to
reinstate 'The glory of manhood' (III, 21) seemed out of
proportion to its grounding in the speaker's experience. In
In Memoriam the move from personal experience to general
'truths' seemed to work because the latter were still, by and

large, within the (marginal and feminine) 'spiritual' realms which poetry was supposed to inhabit; there the danger was that the feminine would get out of hand and threaten customary notions of gender. In *Maud* Tennyson moves to deal with this latter anxiety, making his aggressively heterosexual speaker discover general propositions that are manly, near to the centre of the political process and not merely 'spiritual'. If a true national harmony could be forged out of hostility to foreigners and the idea of a threat to bourgeois freedom, there might be a truly bardic role for the laureate. But it is all too much – hence my suggestion that the poem manifests frustration as well as confidence in the laureate's role.

The paradox is that Tennyson really did want to criticize the ideology of capitalism and imperialism, which aspired to rationalize the cruelty and injustice of the prevailing order. But because he was not prepared to contemplate a radical critique he imagined foreign war to be a resolution. He points out through the speaker that the existing political and economic relations are a kind of civil war:

> But these are the days of advance, the works of the
>   men of mind,
> When who but a fool would have faith in a trades-
>   man's ware or his word?
> Is it peace or war? Civil war, as I think, and that of a
>   kind
> The viler, as underhand, not openly bearing the
>   sword.
>
> (I, 25–8)

Yet he imagines that a foreign war will improve matters ('No more shall commerce be all in all' – III, 23), not seeing that he is merely endorsing a redirection of the violence and injustice endemic in capitalism. He forgets what he knew when he wrote 'Anacaona', 'You ask me, why, though ill at ease' and 'Locksley Hall' – that violence and oppression exported from the centre to the margins are still violence and oppression; that war is not an alternative to capitalism and imperialism but an extension of them. He will not contemplate the fundamental analysis undertaken for instance by Shelley. That *Maud*'s critique was misdirected because of a blockage in its political argument was appreciated by some commentators, and especially by Goldwin Smith writing in 1855 in the *Saturday Review*. The attitude to war, he says, 'appears to be bloodthirstiness, because it is unconnected with any general activity of political or social aspirations. In Milton, Byron, Shelley, Wordsworth, a passionate cry for a just war would have seemed like the foam on the wave – in Mr Tennyson it seems a little like the foam without the wave' (*Critical Heritage*, pp. 189–90).

At the same time, the war is not even a credible resolution – it is improbable that 'the smooth-faced snubnosed rogue would leap from his counter and till,/And strike' (I, 51–2). Because he will not set himself radically at odds with the dominant ideology Tennyson cannot focus his hostility, only strike out in frustration. Presumably the hero of *Maud* will be killed ('The Charge of the Light Brigade' is later in the same volume): the war is a pulling down of the building upon his own head. Goldwin Smith partly sees this too – he points out that Tennyson's characters are often 'wanting in the power of action and active sympathies' (*Critical Heritage*, p. 188). But this is not just a personal failure: Smith has his finger on the limitations upon the role of poetry as it had been constructed around Tennyson from the time of the reviews of Wilson, Fox and Hallam. The poet is not supposed to be active, to interfere in things that matter; he is supposed to cultivate 'spiritual' states of mind or to represent the virtues of bourgeois freedom. The foreign war, which will destroy Tennyson's speaker and many compatriots (let alone those from other countries), is both a way of hitting out in frustration at the whole system and a search for a focus of national harmony. This latter would afford a bardic role to the poet but, in a class society, that role can only thus meretriciously be contrived. The accuracy of this analysis is borne out, I think, by the point at which Smith's argument collapses. He admits that the poet has not an obviously manly role, but his answer is revealingly limp: Tennyson 'has too much sense and solidity of intellect not to know that the manhood of a poet, if it is a little compromised by the softness of his calling, must be redeemed, not by talking lightly of blood, but by true tenderness, self-control, obedience to the moral law, and fidelity to the end of his mission' (p. 189). The vague 'mission' Smith is ready to allow the poet offers no active role for the poet; he cannot conceive of one that will not lead back to the inflammatory Shelleyan conjunction of imaginative and political freedom.

The Sage and the Intellectual

> thou
> Mayst haply learn the Nameless hath a voice,
> By which thou wilt abide, if thou be wise.

So the Ancient Sage (lines 33–5): Tennyson's use of this figure epitomizes one possible stance in the processes of cultural production – bardic authority, claiming to speak a centrist language of universal validity which transcends history and politics, requiring acquiescence ('thou wilt abide, if thou be wise'). This, I have argued, is the role towards which Tennyson was pressured by the culture of his time, though its contradictions could not be suppressed altogether. Opposition to Tennyson in the late Victorian period from what Heyck recognizes as alienated intellectuals invites us to envisage an alternative stance from which to intervene in the prevailing ideological formation.

Tennyson's aspirations to a centrist wisdom long predate the laureateship. In 'Of old sat Freedom on the heights' 'freedom' is linked with 'wisdom' as a way of controlling the Shelleyan implications of freedom (see pp. 27–9 above). In 'Hail Briton!' he proposed an opposition between wisdom and knowledge (lines 129–44) and he developed this in *In*

Memoriam (114). Here knowledge is said to be 'earthly of the mind,/But Wisdom heavenly of the soul' – the standard metaphysical put-down. Knowledge is characterized by a rash disregard for customary pieties:

> Half-grown as yet, a child, and vain –
>   She cannot fight the fear of death.
>   What is she, cut from love and faith,
> But some wild Pallas from the brain
>
> Of Demons? fiery-hot to burst
>   All barriers in her onward race
>   For power.

All kinds of secular enquiry seem to be comprised here, presented so as to discourage radical challenge to established ideas. What is at stake is the possibility of a responsible stance from which a principled political critique of centrist wisdom might be conducted.

It would be tidy if we could derive an alternative position from the young sceptic in 'The Ancient Sage', but Tennyson again slants the argument by making the representative of naturalism merely a voluptuary; he does the same thing in 'Lucretius'. If we reach beyond this, to John Tyndall, in part the model for Tennyson's sceptic (*Memoir*, pp. 815–20), we find a more promising stance. In his notorious Belfast Address as president of the British Association for the Advancement of Science (1874) Tyndall asserted 'scientific naturalism' over against conventional religion, and propounded a principle of intellectual rigour which is liable to threaten ancient sages, metaphysical ploys, and received wisdom generally: 'there is in the true man of science a desire stronger than the wish to have his beliefs upheld; namely the desire to have them true. And this stronger wish causes him to reject the most plausible support, if he has reason to suspect that it is vitiated by error.'[37] Such vigilance in the face of convenient and apparently persuasive ideas – such suspicion of demands to 'abide, if thou be wise' – is what I would set against bardic authority. Unfortunately, upon closer inspection Tyndall's idea of 'science' proves nearly as much of an ideal construction as Tennyson's 'faith',[38] and many of his opinions coincided with Tennyson's (both were in favour of Gordon's attempt to suppress the Sudan and defended Governor Eyre's slaughter of the people of Jamaica). However, there were late Victorian intellectuals who made a distinct break with bourgeois ideology and, like Shelley at the start of Tennyson's life, fought against class and sexual oppression – for instance, William Morris, Eleanor Marx, Edward Carpenter, Olive Schreiner, R. B. Cunninghame Graham.[39]

I am calling the alternative to the Sage the Intellectual though, properly considered, intellectuals should be defined by their role in the relations of production, and there is no necessary link between them and radical thought. They are 'people whose activity is primarily that of elaborating and disseminating ideas'.[40] Thus defined (following Gramsci), they may stand in diverse relationships with the hegemonic class or fraction (Heyck's distinction between men of letters and intellectuals would be better phrased as between incorporated and unincorporated intellectuals). Nevertheless, since the late 1950s, as Alvin Gouldner argues, intellectuals generally have developed a distinctive habit of mind: he calls it a 'culture of critical discourse . . . in which there is nothing that speakers will on principle permanently refuse to discuss or make problematic'.[41] To be sure, what is going on in this apparently critical discourse is often merely complacent or manipulative. Nevertheless, in some institutions at least, including education and 'the arts', it is a discourse through which a genuinely radical political critique may be developed. Intellectuals may stand against bardic authority in modern western culture.

It is sad to observe that during the twentieth century intellectuals specifically involved with Literature have been more vulnerable than most to incorporation by the dominant, and tendencies to the right of the dominant. Literary culture has got itself locked into the belief that it was more highly regarded formerly, and would do better if it could restrain the rate of cultural change in modern society (ironically enough, this is probably not so – writing and reading, and writing and reading about writing and reading, flourish as rarely before). With this in mind, literary culture succumbs easily to the temptation to assert that the writers it features are sages whose work transcends history and politics, and this idea proves generally more compatible with dominant or residual attitudes than with radical ones.

Several qualifications must at once be admitted. First, few academic critics regard their poets as sages in the sense that Tennyson cultivated; already by the end of Tennyson's career, as I have shown, that was not a credible move in intellectual circles. In the prevailing mode, Literature is supposed, rather, to be indirect and understated, requiring special sensitivity for its appreciation. Tennyson's straight-forward bardic stance has become an embarrassment and it either must be rejected or, better still, underlying ambiguity, irony, paradox, indirection, multivalency or polyphony must be discovered. This was a necessary fall-back position, given the manifest marginality of Literature in bourgeois ideology. None the less, through this veil of self-effacement the author and text are treated as sagacious – as uniquely in control of language and as transcending politics and history through the completeness of their 'vision' and their engagement with 'human' values. It is through this assumption that a critical practice whose watchwords are 'discrimination', 'analysis' and 'discussion' in fact refuses questions about the basis of its own operations and, with that, sets beyond its reach the major questions which confront humankind. Furthermore, intellectuals know that Literature is not *actually* a bardic vehicle of central values in modern society – that it no longer has the role which the state and the market combined, briefly and at a cost, to confer upon Tennyson's poetry. Instead its sagacious status is offered as an ideal truth to be grasped by the initiated (who themselves thereby approach sagacity).

Its values are said to transcend particular spatial and temporal locations partly *because* they are known not to prevail in current society: the eternal verities are those which a culture supposedly unsympathetic to Literature neglects. Since the main way to promote Literature and the eternal verities is said to be the reading and teaching of Literature (rather, say, than a study of the configurations of modern culture and of the pressures upon it), the situation is self-fulfilling. What is produced is the indefinite continuation of a sometimes embattled but mostly complacent minority, convinced of the elite quality of a certain range of texts and insights (mainly to do with metaphysics, lately anti-metaphysics, and a limited notion of interpersonal relationships) and preoccupied to the exclusion of almost everything else with protecting its self-image.

For the sage was prepared, at least on occasions, to address the political and social issues which crucially influence the course of human lives. The twentieth-century literary intellectual, defensively withdrawn to supposedly literary topics, is inhibited from handling such matters, and from developing the radical critique – alert to the strategies of power – which we should require of the intellectual.

The situation is now changing (and so producing books like this one), because the dominant construction of Literature has been losing conviction for the most important section of those at whom it is aimed, namely the young who are supposed to benefit from a training in it and to sustain it in the future. The most obvious reason is the competition from other cultural forms; literary culture has by and large failed in its attempt to stigmatize other modes as intolerably vulgar and commercial. Also, the women's movement has made it difficult to take straightforwardly many established texts (almost all?) on account of their sexism – in this respect, however much they knew about 'human' values, our forefathers (occasionally mothers) seem to have got it wrong. Furthermore, a degree of class mobility through the education system has combined with unemployment to make it apparent that a training in

Literature is no longer a preparation for *rule*: it is not a preliminary to joining the governing class. It is above all for this reason that the reading of Literature may now be reconstituted as a technique of suspicion. The sage is inappropriate because sagacity is (allegedly) centrist, and whilst the centre is not yet falling apart, it is not for joining. This is the opportunity for the intellectual to develop techniques for seeing through what those in power are telling us, have been telling us for centuries.

Of course, such an enterprise does not demand attention to Literature; there are lots of other ways of pursuing it. But Literature and its study are places where meanings are made at the moment, and there is no reason to neglect them. It must be remembered, though, that to intervene here requires intelligence and hard work, especially on history and theory (including social and political theory), for simply to complain that a text is idealist or sexist is not to exert influence but to vacate the ground.

In the case of Tennyson, I have tried to show that he was caught up in institutions far beyond the literary, and positioned in ways which were unsatisfactory and contra-dictory, and that the confusions into which this led him are more interesting and illuminating than his affirmations – or those which criticism customarily derives from him. In various ways, at least if we are reading for it, the poems stimulate a radical wariness – through the complex evocation of the imaginative and political status of remote places, the disturbance of poetic voice in dramatic mono-logue, the unconventional handling of gender in *In Memoriam*, the provocative excesses of *Maud*. In a famous passage Walter Benjamin pointed out that 'cultural treasures . . . owe their existence not only to the efforts of the great minds and talents who have created them, but also to the anonymous toil of their contemporaries. There is no document of civilization which is not at the same time a document of barbarism.'[42] However, criticism need not despair of this situation. 'Literature from below' is a phrase used to denote the writings of lower-class people whose work does not normally get classed as Literature. We now need *criticism from below*: an activity which aims not to help the established text into sagacious coherence and accept-ability but to promote awareness of the ideological strategies it may effect and to maintain a shrewd and principled vigilance against them.

Notes

Chapter 1 The Relevance of Tennyson

1 *Alfred Lord Tennyson: A Memoir by His Son* [Hallam Tennyson], 1 vol. (London: Macmillan, 1899), pp. 238, 407, 338. Referred to subsequently in the text as *Memoir*.

2 John D. Jump, ed., *Tennyson: The Critical Heritage* (London: Routledge, 1967), p. 146; from the *Edinburgh Review*, 77, April 1843.

3 Tennyson, *The Lady of Shalott* [and other poems], ed. F. J. Rowe and W. T. Webb (London: Macmillan, 1938), p. xiv.

4 Clyde de L. Ryals, *From the Great Deep: Essays on 'Idylls of the King'* (Ohio University Press, 1967), p. 200.

5 See Jonathan Dollimore, *Radical Tragedy: Religion, Ideology and Power in the Drama of Shakespeare and his Contemporaries* (Brighton: Harvester, 1984), pp. 155–8, 189–95, chapter 16. For Christianity in Ryals' approach, see *From the Great Deep*, p. 199.

6 Cleanth Brooks, *The Well Wrought Urn*, 2nd edn (London: Methuen, 1968), pp. 166–7.

7 See *Memoir*, p. 469; Ryals, *From the Great Deep*, p. 171, also pp. 147–8. Martin, in his recent biography, also rather plays the matter down: 'Alfred, though he never liked the Roman Church itself, became surprisingly tolerant of the faith of its members', Robert Bernard Martin, *Tennyson: The Unquiet Heart* (Oxford University Press, 1980), p. 380. Cf. p. 513.

8 J. H. Plumb, ed., *Crisis in the Humanities* (Harmondsworth: Penguin, 1964), p. 104.

9 See further Jonathan Dollimore and Alan Sinfield, eds, *Political Shakespeare* (Manchester University Press, 1985), chapter 8.

10 Tennyson's poems are quoted from *The Poems of Tennyson*, ed. Christopher Ricks (London: Longmans, 1969); referred to subsequently in the text as Ricks, *Poems*. Quoted here is the 1855 version of part III, line 50 (Ricks, p. 1092).

11 Jerome H. Buckley, *Tennyson: The Growth of a Poet* (Harvard University Press, 1960), p. 142. For further comment on the status of the speaker in *Maud*, see below, pp. 168–74. The evidence that Tennyson thought the Crimean War good for people is substantial; see Martin, *Tennyson*, pp. 381–2.

12 See further Alan Sinfield, 'Four ways with a reactionary text', *LTP* (*Journal of Literature Teaching Politics*), 2 (1983), 81–95; S. Hall, J. Clarke, T. Jefferson and B. Roberts, 'Subcultures, cultures and class', in *Resistance Through Rituals*, ed. Stuart Hall and Tony Jefferson (London: Hutchinson and Centre for Contemporary Cultural Studies, 1976).

13 *Memoir*, pp. 100, 524, 554.

14 Frank Lentricchia, *Criticism and Social Change* (Chicago University Press, 1983), p. 12. See further Tony Bennett, 'Text and history', in *Re-Reading English*, ed. Peter Widdowson (London: Methuen, 1982); Raman Selden, *Criticism and Objectivity* (London: Allen & Unwin, 1984), chapters 1, 7; Iain Wright, 'History, hermeneutics, deconstruction', in *Criticism and Critical Theory*, ed. Jeremy Hawthorn (London: Arnold, 1984).

Chapter 2   The Politics of Poetry

1 W. B. Yeats, *Selected Criticism*, ed. Norman Jeffares (London: Macmillan, 1964), p. 170; W. H. Auden, *Collected Shorter Poems 1927–1957* (London: Faber, 1966), p. 142; Mill's *Essays on Literature and Society*, ed. J. B. Schneewind (New York: Collier, 1965), p. 109.

2 In Isobel Armstrong, ed., *Victorian Scrutinies* (London: Athlone, 1972), p. 109. This volume is cited in the text subsequently as 'Armstrong'. On the explicit political stance of reviewing journals see John Gross, *The Rise and Fall of the Man of Letters* (London: Weidenfeld, 1969), chapter 1.

3 See Jane P. Tompkins, 'The reader in history: the changing shape of literary response', in *Reader-Response Criticism*, ed. Jane P. Tompkins (Baltimore and London: Johns Hopkins, 1980), especially p. 214.

4 *Peacock's Four Ages of Poetry, Shelley's Defence of Poetry, Browning's Essay on Shelley*, ed. H. F. B. Brett-Smith (Oxford: Blackwell, 1947), p. 24. Shelley's *Defence* was not published until 1840 but his ideas were already influential through the poems: see Lionel Stevenson, 'Tennyson, Browning and a Romantic fallacy', *University of Toronto Quarterly*, 13 (1944), 175–95.

5 See Paul Foot, *Red Shelley* (London: Sidgwick & Jackson, 1980); John Lucas, 'Politics and the poet's role', in *Literature and Politics in the Nineteenth Century*, ed. John Lucas (London: Methuen, 1971).

6 E. P. Thompson, 'The peculiarities of the English', in *The Poverty of*

Theory and Other Essays (London: Merlin Press, 1978), p. 73: quoting Gwyn A. Williams, 'The concept of "egemonia" in the thought of Antonio Gramsci', *Journal of the History of Ideas*, 21 (1960), 586–99. See also Chantal Mouffe, 'Hegemony and ideology in Gramsci', in *Culture, Ideology and Social Process*, ed. Tony Bennett et al. (London: Batsford and Open University, 1981).

7 See Thompson, 'The peculiarities of the English', in *The Poverty of Theory*, pp. 42–56, 62–4, 72–4; Robert Gray, 'Bourgeois hegemony in Victorian Britain', in *The Communist University of London: Papers on Class, Hegemony and Party*, ed. Jon Bloomfield (London: Lawrence & Wishart, 1977), reprinted in *Culture, Ideology and Social Process*, ed. Bennett et al.; Barry Supple, 'The governing framework: social class and institutional reform in Victorian Britain', in *The Victorians*, ed. Laurence Lerner (London: Methuen, 1978).

8 Charles Babbage, *On the Economy of Manufactures* (London: Charles Knight, 1832), pp. 15, 17.

9 *Manifesto of the Communist Party*, in Karl Marx, *The Revolutions of 1848*, ed. David Fernbach (Harmondsworth: Penguin, 1973), p. 83.

10 Martin, *Tennyson*, pp. 462–3.

11 Hume and Ure are quoted from *Class and Conflict in Nineteenth-century England 1815–1850*, ed. Patricia Hollis (London: Routledge, 1973), pp. 352, 344.

12 Thomas Carlyle, *Signs of the Times*, in *Selected Writings*, ed. Alan Shelston (Harmondsworth: Penguin, 1971), p. 73; Lord [Thomas Babington] Macaulay, *Essays, Historical and Literary* (London: Ward, Lock, n.d.), p. 3. See Armstrong, pp. 15–8; Raman Selden, *Criticism and Objectivity* (London: Allen & Unwin, 1984), pp. 14–21; Patrick Parrinder, *Authors and Authority* (London: Routledge, 1977), pp. 104–16.

13 *Westminster Review*, 4 (July 1825), 166, quoted by Walter E. Houghton, *The Victorian Frame of Mind 1830–1870* (Yale University Press, 1957), p. 115. See generally Houghton, pp. 110–24 and Richard D. Altick, *The English Common Reader* (Chicago University Press, 1963), chapter 6.

14 See Selden, *Criticism and Objectivity*, pp. 18–9.

15 Parrinder, *Authors and Authority*, p. 86.

16 Harold Bloom, *Poetry and Repression* (Yale University Press, 1976), p. 4.

17 Edgar Finley Shannon, Jr, *Tennyson and the Reviewers* (Cambridge, Mass.: Harvard University Press, 1952), p. 22. See also Stevenson, 'Tennyson, Browning, and a Romantic fallacy'; and Margaret A. Lourie, 'Below the thunders of the upper deep: Tennyson as a Romantic revisionist', *Studies in Romanticism*, 18 (1979), 3–27.

18 *The Complete Poetical Works of Percy Bysshe Shelley*, ed. Thomas Hutchinson (Oxford University Press, 1943), 'Ode to Liberty', stanza 11.

19 Frederick Denison Maurice, *Sketches of Contemporary Authors, 1828*, ed. A. J. Hartley (New York: Archon, 1970), p. 72.

20 See Shannon, *Tennyson and the Reviewers*, pp. 7, 13–4.

21 Martin, *Tennyson*, p. 120.

22 E. J. Hobsbawm, *The Age of Revolution* (London: Weidenfeld, 1962), p. 105. On the revolutions of this period see chapter 6.

23 Charles Tennyson, *Six Tennyson Essays* (London: Cassell, 1954), p. 41.

24 Hollis, *Class and Conflict*, pp. 67–8.

25 J. L. and Barbara Hammond, *The Village Labourer*, 2 vols. (London: Longmans for Guild Books, 1948), II, 46.

26 Hammonds, *Village Labourer*, II, 98.

27 Babbage, *On the Economy of Manufactures*, pp. 229–30.

28 Tennyson, *Six Tennyson Essays*, p. 40. See also Martin, *Tennyson*, p. 125.

29 E. J. Hobsbawm and George Rudé, *Captain Swing* (London: Lawrence & Wishart, 1970), pp. 262–3; on Cambridge see pp. 165–7.

30 Quoted in E. P. Thompson, *The Making of the English Working Class*, 2nd edn. (London: Gollancz, 1980), p. 899.

31 Hollis, *Class and Conflict*, p. 75.

32 Thompson, *The Making of the English Working Class*, p. 898.

33 Quoted by Thompson, *The Making of the English Working Class*, p. 905.

34 R. W. Postgate, *Revolution from 1789 to 1906* (London: Grant Richards, 1920), p. 118. See also Hollis, *Class and Conflict*, p. 75; and Dorothy Thompson, ed., *The Early Chartists* (University of South Carolina Press, 1971), p. 150.

35 Hollis, *Class and Conflict*, p. 194. See also Postgate, *Revolution from 1789 to 1906*, p. 91.

36 See George Lichtheim, *Imperialism* (Harmondsworth, 1971), pp. 49–52.

37 Hobsbawm, *Age of Revolution*, p. 150. See also Hobsbawm and Rudé, *Captain Swing*, chapter 2.

38 Hollis, *Class and Conflict*, p. 147. See further Thompson, *The Making of the English Working Class*, pp. 799–806; and Donald Read, *Press and People* (London: Arnold, 1961).

39 Marx, *Revolutions of 1848*, p. 82.

40 Quoted in W. D. Paden, *Tennyson in Egypt* (University of Kansas Publications, 1942), p. 67.

41 See Paden, *Tennyson in Egypt*, pp. 145–8.

42 *The Journals of Captain James Cook on His Voyages of Discovery*, ed. J. C. Beaglehole, 2 vols. (Hakluyt Society and Cambridge University Press, 1955, 1961), I, 76.

43 *The 'Endeavour' Journal of Joseph Banks, 1768–1771*, ed. J. C. Beaglehole, 2 vols. (Public Library of New South Wales and Angus and Robertson, 1962), I, 252.

44 *Journals of Captain Cook*, I, 114–16, II, 404; Alan Moorehead, *The Fatal Impact* (London: Hamish Hamilton, 1966), pp. 76–7, 88, 94–5.

45 *The Life and Voyages of Christopher Columbus*, 2 vols., *The Works of Washington Irving* (London: Bell, 1896), II, 567.

46 Irving, *Life and Voyages of Columbus*, II, 902, 906.

47 Quoted in Paden, *Tennyson in Egypt*, p. 68.

48 Marx, *Revolutions of 1848*, p. 71.

49 John Stuart Mill, *Principles of Political Economy* (London: Longmans, Green, 1909), pp. 581–2.

50 Hobsbawm, *Age of Revolution*, p. 165; see also p. 35.

51 Hobsbawm, *Age of Revolution*, p. 107.

52 Irving, *Life and Voyages of Columbus*, I, 124, 372.

53 *'Endeavour' Journal of Joseph Banks*, I, 252.

54 Louis de Bougainville, *A Voyage Round the World* (Amsterdam: N. Israel; New York: Da Capo; London: Frank Cass, 1967), pp. 218–19.

55 Edward W. Said, *Orientalism* (London: Routledge, 1978), p. 150.

56 Irving, *Life and Voyages of Columbus*, II, 600, 606.

57 Francis T. Palgrave, ed., *The Golden Treasury*, Complete Edition (London: Macmillan, 1909), p. x. Cf. *Memoir*, pp. 842–4.

58 See C. K. Stead, *The New Poetic* (London: Hutchinson, 1964).

59 H. M. McLuhan, 'Tennyson and Picturesque Poetry', in *Critical Essays on the Poetry of Tennyson*, ed. John Killham (London: Routledge, 1960); Frank Kermode, *Romantic Image* (London: Routledge, 1957).

60 Gérard Genette, 'Valéry and the Poetics of Language', in *Textual Strategies*, ed. Josué V. Harari (London: Methuen, 1980), p. 364.

61 T. S. Eliot, *Selected Prose*, ed. John Hayward (Harmondsworth: Peregrine, 1963), p. 110.

62 I. A. Richards, *Principles of Literary Criticism*, 2nd edn. (London: Routledge, 1926), p. 33.

Chapter 3 'The Mortal Limits of the Self'

1 Lines 229–39. Cf. A. Dwight Culler, *The Poetry of Tennyson* (Yale University Press, 1977), pp. 1–8.

2 Plotinus, *The Enneads*, trans. Stephen MacKenna, 4th edn, revised B. S. Page (London: Faber, 1969), IV. 8, p. 357.

3 On Saussure, see Terence Hawkes, *Structuralism and Semiotics* (London: Methuen, 1977).

4 On Lacan, see *Feminine Sexuality: Jacques Lacan and the école freudienne*, ed. Juliet Mitchell and Jacqueline Rose (London: Macmillan, 1982).

5 Jacques Derrida, *Writing and Difference*, trans. Alan Bass (London: Routledge, 1978), p. 292.

6 *The Poetical Works of Robert Browning*, 1833–1858, 2 vols (London: Hutchinson, 1906), II, 510.

7 See Kerry McSweeney, *Tennyson and Swinburne as Romantic Naturalists* (Toronto University Press, 1981), p. 21.

8 Derrida, *Writing and Difference*, p. 19; *Of Grammatology*, trans. Gayatri Chakravorty Spivak (Johns Hopkins University Press, 1976), p. 315.

9 William Walsh, *The Use of Imagination* (Harmondsworth: Peregrine, 1966), p. 180. Walsh aims to correct a tendency in this view not to take into account the 'potential and dynamic nature' of character.

10 Juliet Mitchell in *Feminine Sexuality*, p. 5.

11 In *Tennyson: Writers and their Background*, ed. D. J. Palmer (London: Bell, 1973), p. 28.

12 Jacqueline Rose in *Feminine Sexuality*, p. 30.

13 Harold Nicolson, *Tennyson: Aspects of his Life, Character and Poetry* (London: Grey Arrow Books, 1960), p. 34.

14 Martin, *Tennyson*, p. 277; also pp. 27–9, 83–5, 238, 278–80.

15 This section seems to derive from Arthur Hallam's essay 'On Sympathy': in *The Writings of Arthur Hallam*, ed. T. H. Vail Motter (New York: Modern Language Association of America, 1943; Oxford University Press, 1943), pp. 134, 137. Its Lacanian properties are noted by Terry Eagleton in 'Tennyson: Politics and Sexuality in *The Princess* and *In Memoriam*', in *1848: The Sociology of Literature*, ed. Francis Barker et al. (University of Essex, 1978), p. 104. See also, on infants and language, *In Memoriam* 54 and 124.

16 Geoffrey Hartman, *Saving the Text* (Johns Hopkins University Press, 1981), p. 97.

Chapter 4   Strategies of Language and Subjectivity

1 Alan Sinfield, *The Language of Tennyson's 'In Memoriam'* (Oxford: Blackwell, 1971), p. 5.

2 *Style in Language*, ed. Thomas A. Sebeok (Cambridge, Mass.: MIT Press, 1960), pp. 377, 371.

3 Sinfield, *The Language of Tennyson's 'In Memoriam'*, p. 7.

4 Jonathan Culler, *Structuralist Poetics* (London: Routledge, 1971), p. 161 and chapter 8 generally.

5 J. M. Gray, *Tennyson's Doppelgänger: Balin and Balan* (Lincoln: The Tennyson Society, 1971), p. 26.

6 *Sound and Poetry*, English Institute Essays, 1956 (Columbia University Press, 1957), p. xiv.

7 E. L. Epstein, *Language and Style* (London: Methuen, 1978), p. 37.

8 Quoted in Ricks, *Poems*, p. 743, with reference to *The Princess*, conclusion, line 6.

9 Walter Bagehot, *Literary Studies*, 3 vols (London: Longmans, Green, 1898), II, 353.

10 *The Major Victorian Poets: Reconsiderations*, ed. Isobel Armstrong (London: Routledge, 1969), p. 10.

11 Antony Easthope, *Poetry as Discourse* (London: Methuen, 1983), pp. 124–5.

12 Richard Rorty, 'Philosophy as a kind of writing: an essay on Derrida', *New Literary History*, 10 (1978), 141–60, p. 146.

13 For the 1833 version of 'Early Spring' see Ricks, *Poems*, pp. 496–8; for the 1983 version see pp. 1314–16.

14 *The Letters of Alfred Lord Tennyson*, ed. Cecil Y. Lang and Edgar F. Shannon, Jr, Vol. 1 (Oxford University Press, 1982), p. 173.

15 Gérard Genette, 'Valéry and the poetics of language', in *Textual Strategies*, ed. Josué V. Harari (London: Methuen, 1980), p. 364.

16 A. Dwight Culler, *The Poetry of Tennyson* (Yale University Press, 1977), p. 5. Horne's essay, of 1844, is in *Critical Heritage*, ed. Jump: see p. 155.

17 Roland Barthes, *Mythologies* (St Albans: Paladin, 1973), p. 133.

18 H. M. McLuhan, 'Tennyson and picturesque poetry', in *Critical Essays on the Poetry of Tennyson*, ed. John Killham (London: Routledge, 1960), pp. 70, 75. See also John D. Rosenberg, *The Fall of Camelot* (Harvard University Press, 1973), p. 2 and chapters 4, 6.

19 W. K. Wimsatt, Jr, *The Verbal Icon* (University of Kentucky Press, 1954), pp. 109–10. Cf. Cleanth Brooks' belief, quoted in chapter 1, that the poet's task is 'finally to unify experience' (*Well Wrought Urn*, p. 173).

20 'The rhetoric of temporality' in Paul de Man, *Blindness and Insight*, 2nd edn (London: Methuen, 1983), pp. 188, 206, 207.

21 *The Critical Heritage*, ed. Jump, p. 360.

22 *Blindness and Insight*, p. 207.

23 Paul de Man, *Allegories of Reading* (Yale University Press, 1979), p. 201.

24 W. David Shaw, *Tennyson's Style* (Cornell University Press, 1976), p. 286.

25 Shaw, *Tennyson's Style*, p. 287, quoting Wimsatt, *The Verbal Icon*, p. 115.

26 James J. Sherry, 'Tennyson and the paradox of the sign', *Victorian Poetry*, 17 (1979), 204–16, p. 210. Cf. Christopher Ricks, *Tennyson* (London: Macmillan, 1972), p. 143.

27 De Man, *Allegories of Reading*, p. 204.

28 *Critical Heritage*, ed. Jump, p. 86.

29 Sherry, 'Tennyson and the paradox of the sign', p. 212.

30 De Man, *Blindness and Insight*, p. 208. For the charge that de Man attributes deconstructive awareness unreasonably to the authors he discusses, see P. D. Juhl, 'Playing with texts: can deconstruction account for critical practice?', in *Criticism and Critical Theory*, ed. Hawthorn.

31 Jacques Derrida, *Speech and Phenomenon*, trans. David B. Alison (Evanston, Ill., 1972), pp. 158–9.

32 Anthony Wilden, ed., *The Language of the Self*, by Jacques Lacan (Johns Hopkins University Press, 1968), pp. 163–4.

33 See for instance Kerry McSweeney, *Tennyson and Swinburne as Romantic Naturalists* (University of Toronto, 1981), pp. 69–74; Arthur J. Carr, 'Tennyson as a modern poet', in Killham, ed., *Critical Essays*.

34 Eliot, *Selected Prose*, p. 173.

35 Juliet Mitchell, in *Feminine Sexuality*, ed. Mitchell and Rose, pp. 5–6; see also pp. 30–3.

36 McSweeney, *Tennyson and Swinburne as Romantic Naturalists*, p. 188.

37 De Man, *Blindness and Insight*, p. 200.

38 Culler, *The Poetry of Tennyson*, pp. 42–3.

39 Rosenberg, *The Fall of Camelot*, p. 27; Gray, *Tennyson's Doppelgänger*, p. 9.

40 Alan Sinfield, *Dramatic Monologue* (London: Methuen, 1977), p. 25 and chapter 3 generally. Cf. Käte Hamburger, *The Logic of Literature*, 2nd edn, trans. Marilynn J. Rose (Indiana University Press, 1973).

41 Raman Selden, *Criticism and Objectivity* (London: Allen & Unwin, 1984), pp. 124–5.

42 Robert Langbaum, *The Poetry of Experience* (Harmondsworth: Penguin, 1974), chapter 2.

43 Ricks, *Poems*, p. 1113; quoting M. J. Donahue, 'Tennyson's *Hail Briton!* and *Tithon*', *PMLA*, 64 (1949), 385–416. For an argument that Tennyson's monologues do not fit the Langbaum model see Ralph W. Rader, 'The dramatic monologue and related lyric forms', *Critical Inquiry*, 3 (1976), 131–51.

44 *Roland Barthes by Roland Barthes*, trans. Richard Howard (London: Macmillan, 1977), p. 143. Quoted with permission.

45 Selden, *Criticism and Objectivity*, pp. 143–4.

46 Shaw, *Tennyson's Style*, p. 89.

47 Sinfield, *Dramatic Monologue*, p. 59 and chapter 6 generally.

48 Michel Foucault, *The Order of Things* (London: Tavistock, 1970), p. 305.

Chapter 5   The Importance of Arthur Being

1 On language in the poem, see Peter Allan Dale, '"Gracious Lies": the meaning of metaphor in *In Memoriam*', *Victorian Poetry*, 18 (1980), 147–67.

2 Shannon, *Tennyson and the Reviewers*, p. 147.

3 See Marion Shaw, '*In Memoriam* and popular religious poetry', *Victorian Poetry*, 15 (1977), 1–8.

4 Shannon, *Tennyson and the Reviewers*, pp. 142, 152.

5 Tennyson, *In Memoriam*, ed. Susan Shatto and Marion Shaw (Oxford: Clarendon, 1982), pp. 11–5, 312–5, 317–20.

6 Terry Eagleton, 'Tennyson: politics and sexuality in *The Princess* and *In Memoriam*', in *1848: The Sociology of Literature*, ed. Francis Barker et al. (University of Essex, 1978), p. 104.

7 Quoted in *In Memoriam*, ed. Shatto and Shaw, p. 211.

8 James R. Kincaid, *Tennyson's Major Poems* (Yale University Press, 1975), pp. 105, 109 and chapter 5 generally.

9 McSweeney, *Tennyson and Swinburne as Romantic Naturalists*, p. xiii and chapter 3.

10 Peter Hinchcliffe, 'Elegy and epithalamium in *In Memoriam*', *University of Toronto Quarterly*, 52 (1983), 241–62, pp. 257–9.

11 Macaulay, *Essays, Historical and Literary*, p. 243.

12 Hollis, *Class and Conflict*, p. 208.

13 Cf. Marx and Engels, 'Manifesto of the Communist Party', in Marx, *Revolutions of 1848*, p. 79.

14 Ricks, *Poems*, pp. 859–61; Shatto and Shaw, note 5 above.

15 'An art that will not abandon the self to language: Bloom, Tennyson, and the blind world of the wish', in *Untying the Text: A Post-Structuralist Reader*, ed. Robert Young (London: Routledge, 1981), pp. 218, 216.

16 *Roland Barthes by Roland Barthes*, trans. Richard Howard (London: Macmillan, 1977), p. 148. Quoted with permission.

17 Paul de Man, 'Autobiography as de-facement', *Modern Language Notes*, 94 (1979), 919–30, p. 921.

18 See Shannon, *Tennyson and the Reviewers*, pp. 141–2.

19 Sir Charles Tennyson, *Alfred Tennyson* (London: Macmillan, 1949), p. 336 – quoting the letter sent from the Queen.

20 T. H. Vail Motter, ed., *The Writings of Arthur Hallam* (New York: Modern Language Association of America, 1943; Oxford University Press, 1945), pp. 15–17, 229, 159. See also Gerhard Joseph, *Tennysonian Love: the Strange Diagonal* (University of Minnesota Press, 1969), chapter 4.

21 Stephen Greenblatt, 'Invisible bullets: Renaissance authority and its subversion', in *Political Shakespeare*, ed. Jonathan Dollimore and Alan Sinfield (Manchester University Press, 1985), p. 29.

22 Martin, *Tennyson*, p. 95; and see pp. 94–6, 218–9, 286–7. See also Ralph Wilson Rader, *Tennyson's 'Maud': the Biographical Genesis* (University of California Press, 1963), pp. 144–5 (an endnote).

23 Ricks, *Tennyson*, pp. 216–20. For the Spedding letter see Lang and Shannon, ed., *Letters of Tennyson*, p. 87.

24 Jeffrey Weeks, *Sex, Politics and Society* (London and New York: Longman, 1981), p. 2.

25 Mary Wollstonecraft, *The Rights of Women*, John Stuart Mill, *The Subjection of Women* (London and New York: Everyman's Library, 1929), p. 238; see also pp. 229–30, 273.

26 See Jeffrey Weeks, *Coming Out: Homosexual Politics in Britain* (London, Melbourne and New York: Quartet Books, 1977), p. 3.

27 Michel Foucault, *The History of Sexuality: Volume I: An Introduction*, trans. Robert Hurley (New York: Vintage Books, 1980), p. 36. See also Weeks, *Sex, Politics and Society*, pp. 19–21.

28 Weeks, *Coming Out*, pp. 33–5.

29 Gray, 'Bourgeois hegemony in Victorian Britain', pp. 85–6.

30 Peter T. Cominos, 'Innocent femina sensualis in unconscious conflict', in *Suffer and Be Still*, ed. Martha Vicinus (Indiana University Press, 1972), p.156. For evidence that this position was not unquestioned, see F. Barry Smith, 'Sexuality in Britain, 1800–1900: some suggested revisions', in *A Widening Sphere*, ed. Martha Vicinus (Indiana University Press, 1977).

31 Leonore Davidoff, 'Class and gender in Victorian England', in *Sex and Class in Women's History*, ed. Judith L. Newton, Mary P. Ryan and Judith R. Walkowitz (London: Routledge, 1983), p. 20. See also Weeks, *Sex, Politics and Society*, pp. 38–40.

32 Rader, *Tennyson's 'Maud'*, p. 22; following Sir Charles Tennyson, *Tennyson*, pp. 162–3, and Sir Charles, *Six Tennyson Essays*, p. 102. But cf. Martin, *Tennyson*, pp. 215–21.

33 See Armstrong, *Victorian Scrutinies*, pp. 99–100, 81–2, 118–9; Jump, ed., *Critical Heritage*, pp. 89–90, also p. 115.

34 John Killham, 'Tennyson and social values', in *Tennyson: Writers and their Background*, ed. Palmer, p. 165.

35 Carol Christ, 'Victorian masculinity and the angel in the house', in *A Widening Sphere*, ed. Vicinus, p. 158.

36 See further Robert Gray, 'Bourgeois hegemony in Victorian Britain'; Alan Sinfield, 'Power and ideology: an outline theory and Sidney's *Arcadia*, *ELH*, 52 (1985), 259–77; Jonathan Dollimore, 'Transgression and surveillance in *Measure for Measure*', in Dollimore and Sinfield, eds, *Political Shakespeare* (Manchester University Press, 1985).

37 See Norman Vance, *The Sinews of the Spirit: the Ideal of Christian Manliness in Victorian Literature and Religious Thought* (Cambridge University Press, 1985), Introduction.

38 C. H. Spurgeon, *A Good Start: A Book for Young Men and Women* (1898), quoted in Vance, *Sinews of the Spirit*.

39 Thomas Hughes, *Tom Brown's Schooldays* (London: Dent, 1903), p. 193.

40 See Vance, *Sinews of the Spirit*, chapter 5.

41 Walter Bagehot, *Literary Studies*, II, 380–1.

42 Martin, *Tennyson*, pp. 169 and 169–73.

43 *Critical Heritage*, ed. Jump, p. 81.

44 Quoted by Mark A. Weinstein in *William Edmonstoune Aytoun and the Spasmodic Controversy* (Yale University Press, 1968), pp. 172–3.

45 *Memoir*, p. 157. This was presumably before guardsmen got the reputation of being available to homosexuals. Weeks, *Coming Out*, pp. 35.

46 Christ, 'Victorian masculinity and the angel in the house', pp. 151–2, 155–6.

47 Mill, *The Subjection of Women*, p. 232.

48 Eagleton, 'Tennyson: politics and sexuality', p. 101.

49 *The Times*, 28 November 1851, p. 8. See Nicolson, *Tennyson*, pp. 157–8; Shannon, *Tennyson and the Reviewers*, p. 157.

50 Eliot, *Selected Prose*, p. 170.

51 Foucault, *History of Sexuality: Vol. 1*, pp. 59, 63.

52 Davidoff, 'Class and gender in Victorian England', p. 31.

53 *Greek Pastoral Poetry*, trans. Anthony Holden (Harmondsworth: Penguin, 1974), p. 128.

54 Sigmund Freud, 'Mourning and Melancholia', in Freud, *On Metapsychology: the Theory of Psychoanalysis*, The Pelican Freud Library, vol. 11 (Harmondsworth: Penguin, 1984), p. 254.

55 Weeks, *Coming Out*, chapter 1.

56 Allon White, *The Uses of Obscurity* (London: Routledge, 1981), pp. 46–7. See also Foucault, *The Order of Things*, p. 299 and Foucault, *History of Sexuality: Vol. 1*, p. 69.

Chapter 6   The Laureate in the Market Place

1 Valerie Pitt, *Tennyson Laureate* (London: Barrie & Rockliff, 1962). Cf. Ian Jak, *The Poet and his Audience* (Cambridge University Press, 1984), chapter 5.

2 John Morley, *The Life of William Ewart Gladstone*, 2 vols (London: Edward Lloyd, 1908), II, 267.

3 See Nicolson, *Tennyson*, pp. 210–14; Marion Shaw, 'Tennyson and his his public 1827–1859', in *Tennyson: Writers and their Background*, ed. Palmer, pp. 77–88.

4 June Steffensen Hagen, *Tennyson and his Publishers* (London: Macmillan, 1979), p. 89. See also Martin, *Tennyson*, p. 391.

5 Geoffrey Best, *Mid-Victorian Britain 1851–75* (Glasgow: Fontana/Collins, 1979), p. 246. See also Altick, *The English Common Reader*, p. 295.

6 Hagen, *Tennyson and his Publishers*, p. 112; Martin, *Tennyson*, p. 480.

7 *Revolutions of 1848*, p. 70.

8 Best, *Mid-Victorian Britain*, pp. 250–1; and generally 250–60.

9 Altick, *The Common Reader*, pp. 277, 286.

10 Jane P. Tompkins, *Reader-Response Criticism*, p. 218.

11 Quoted by Shaw, *Tennyson: Writers and their Background*, p. 81.

12 See Edgar F. Shannon, Jr, 'The critical reception of Tennyson's *Maud*', *PMLA*, 68 (1953), 397–417, p. 402.

13 *Critical Heritage*, p. 250. See Armstrong, pp. 51–3.

14 P. G. Scott, *Tennyson's 'Enoch Arden': A Victorian Best-Seller* (Lincoln:

The Tennyson Society, 1970); John Killham, 'Tennyson and Victorian social values', in *Tennyson: Writers and their Background*, p. 156.

15 Matthew Arnold, *Selected Prose*, ed. P. J. Keating (Harmondsworth: Penguin, 1970), p. 121.

16 Quoted by Altick, *The English Common Reader*, p. 198.

17 Sir Charles Tennyson, *Tennyson*, p. 354; and see Hagen, *Publishers*, p. 114.

18 G. M. Young, 'The Age of Tennyson', in *Critical Essays on the Poetry of Tennyson*, ed. Killham, p.27.

19 Best, *Mid-Victorian Britain*, p. 259. See also Thompson, 'Peculiarities of the English' in *The Poverty of Theory*, pp. 53–4.

20 T. W. Heyck, 'From men of letters to intellectuals: the transformation of intellectual life in nineteenth-century England', *Journal of British Studies*, 20 (1980), 158–83.

21 See Shaw in *Tennyson: Writers and their Background*, p. 86.

22 Quoted by Nicolson, *Tennyson*, p. 212.

23 Quoted by Shaw in *Tennyson: Writers and their Background*, p. 53.

24 Jean-Paul Sartre, *What Is Literature?*, trans. Bernard Frechtman (London: Methuen, 1950), p. 88.

25 See Joseph, *Tennysonian Love*, chapter 10; McSweeney, *Tennyson and Swinburne*, chapter 4.

26 Quoted by Shannon, 'The critical reception of Tennyson's *Maud*', p. 413.

27 Foucault, *History of Sexuality: Vol. I*, pp. 124–5.

28 John Killham, 'Tennyson's *Maud* – the function of the imagery', in *Critical Essays*, ed. Killham; Ann C. Colley, *Tennyson and Madness* (University of Georgia Press, 1983), pp. 84–5. See also pp. 7–8 and chapter 1, note 11.

29 Ricks, *Tennyson*, pp. 246–7; Rader, *Tennyson's 'Maud'*, chapter 4.

30 Ricks, *Tennyson*, pp. 254, 263; Philip Drew, 'Tennyson and the dramatic monologue: a study of *Maud*', in *Tennyson: Writers and their Background*, pp. 137–8. However, Ricks also makes a comparison with Beckett's *Krapp's Last Tape* in a footnote (p. 249): cf. p. 109 above.

31 *Memoir*, p. 339. On Mann, see Culler, *The Poetry of Tennyson*, pp. 200–2.

32 Quoted in Weinstein, *William Edmonstoune Aytoun*, p. 179.

33 In *Tennyson: Writers and their Background*, p. 124.

34 Lang and Shannon, eds, *Letters of Tennyson*, p. 239.

35 Lionel Stevenson, 'The "high-born maiden" symbol in Tennyson', in *Critical Essays*, ed. Killham, p. 136. Cf. Joseph, *Tennysonian Love*, pp. 52–4, 104, 116.

36 Sir Charles Tennyson: 'Tennyson as poet laureate', in *Tennyson: Writers and their Background*, p. 217. See also Culler, *The Poetry of Tennyson*, p. 205, and Gladstone's review of *Idylls of the King* (1859), *Critical Heritage*, p. 247.

37 A. S. Eve and C. H. Creasey, *Life and Work of John Tyndall* (London: Macmillan, 1945), p. 184.

38 See Frank M. Turner, 'John Tyndall and Victorian Scientific Naturalism', in *John Tyndall: Essays on a Natural Philosopher*, ed. W. H. Brock, N. D. McMillan and R. C. Mollan (Dublin: Royal Dublin Society, 1981).

39 See E. P. Thompson, *William Morris: Romantic to Revolutionary*, 2nd edn. (London: Merlin, 1977); Cedric Watts and Laurence Davies, *Cunninghame Graham* (Cambridge University Press, 1979); Sheila Rowbotham and Jeffrey Weeks, *Socialism and the New Life* (London: Pluto Press, 1977); Ruth First and Ann Scott, *Olive Schreiner* (London: Deutsch, 1980).

40 Erik Olin Wright, 'Intellectuals and the class structure of capitalist society', in *Between Capital and Labour*, ed. Pat Walker (Hassocks: Harvester, 1979), p. 192.

41 Alvin W. Gouldner, *The Future of Intellectuals and the Rise of the New Class* (London: Macmillan, 1979), p. 28. See further *Political Shakespeare*, ed. Dollimore and Sinfield, chapters 8 and 9.

42 Walter Benjamin, *Illuminations*, ed. Hannah Arendt, trans. Harry Zohn (Glasgow: Fontana/Collins, 1973), p. 258.

Index